THE
GLORY OF
GOD

THE
GLORY OF
GOD

Compiled by Eugene Carvalho

The Glory of God

Copyright © 2019 by Eugene Carvalho

ISBN: 9781091603240

Printed in the United States of America

To the Body of Christ.
May this compilation bless you richly!
With love…

TABLE OF CONTENTS

PURPOSE AND ACKNOWLEDGEMENTS

The infallible Word of God for faith and conduct informs us that the Holy Spirit gives gifts to men and women of the Body of Christ. It states: "the gifts edify the body for the building up of the saints" (Eph. 4:12). I hope the talents and gifts the Lord has given me will be a blessing to someone else through the reading of this compilation.

I am grateful for the love from all family members, especially my wife Mercedes Carvalho. I am also grateful for the knowledge, wisdom and love of many pastors, teachers, and saints that the Lord has used to bless me. Lastly, I must not forget a special thank you to my friend Kathryn Regan for proofreading this material.

Chapter One
THE GLORY OF GOD

In my studies in Bible college one of my favorite topics in the Old Testament was the glory of God. Moses asked God to show him His glory. The Bible says, "And he said, I beseech thee, shew me thy glory. And He said, I will make all my goodness pass before thee, and I will proclaim the name of the Lord before thee; and will be gracious to whom I will be gracious, and will shew mercy on whom I will shew mercy. And He said, thou canst not see My face: for there shall no man see Me, and live. And the Lord said, behold, there is a place by Me, and thou shalt stand upon a rock: and it shall come to pass, while My glory passeth by, that I will put thee in a clift of the rock, and will cover thee with My hand while I pass by: and I will take away mine hand, and thou shalt see My back parts: but My face shall not be seen" (Ex. 33:18-23 KJV).

Moses wanted God's glory while the rest of the congregation was at the bottom of the mountain messing around with idolatry. Maybe much of the church today is the same way. Some individuals may want the ministers to fast and pray and study hard for the services and sermons while they play with their television and cell phones.

"Since the close of the Old Testament, the glory of God has been shown mainly in Christ (Luke 9:29-32; John 2:11) and in members of His church. Christ now shares His divine glory with His followers (John 17:5-6, 22), so that in their lives Christians are being transformed into the glorious image of God (2 Cor. 3:18). Believers will be fully glorified at the end of time in God's heavenly presence (Ro. 5:2; Col. 3:4). There the glory of God will be seen everywhere (Rev. 21:23)."[1]

You should be shouting and waking everybody up in the house after hearing that, "The glory of God will be seen everywhere." That's powerful stuff!

As you may know by now, I truly enjoy winning souls in the street of Mexico. Individuals that pray with me to receive Christ, as their personal Lord and Savior, are transformed. After a few minutes many times you can see the glory of God come on them. Their faces and eyes start shining. They are transformed from darkness into marvelous light and receive God's glory.

I want to share an experience I had this morning at 4 AM. I was in my recliner reading my Bible and my puppy Toby came over and wanted my attention. So I put him on my lap and was running my fingers through his very thick fur. When we first got him in Veracruz, Mexico, the vet cut his hair so close and since then he's like a big ball of fur, which, means it's time for him to get a haircut.

I got a revelation how the fur was covering him and protecting him and how God created all His creation with covering. Man is God's only creation that wears clothes for covering. The fish have scales for covering. The elephant and hippo have hide and the birds have feathers. God also created man with covering. Adam was created and covered with the glory of God but when he sinned the glory departed

---

[1] Thomas Nelson, *Nelson's New Illustrated Bible Dictionary* (Nashville: Thomas Nelson Publishers, 1995), p. 449.

from him. Then Adam realized he was naked and had no covering, so he covered himself with fig leaves.

Adam was crowned with God's glory and he wore it as a crown and clothing. David, my favorite psalmists, wrote, "What is man that You take thought of him, and the son of man that You care for him? Yet You have made him a little lower than God, and You crown him with glory and majesty" (Ps. 8:4-5)![2]

When an individual receives Jesus and is born-again they receive God's glory. The Bible says, "For by grace you have been saved through faith; and that not of yourselves, it is the gift of God; not as a result of works, so that no one may boast" (Eph. 2:8).

Apostle Paul, one of the greatest minds of western civilization ever saw, wrote the following, "But we all, with unveiled face, beholding as in a mirror the glory of the Lord, are being transformed into the same image from glory to glory, just as from the Lord, the Spirit" (2 Cor. 3:18).

God has called His people (the Church) to increase from glory to glory. Here's what Paul writes concerning the aforementioned, "Now I rejoice in my sufferings for your sake, and in my flesh I do my share on behalf of His body, which is the church, in filling up what is lacking in Christ's afflictions. Of this church I was made a minister according to the stewardship from God bestowed on me for your benefit, so that I might fully carry out the preaching

---

[2] All Scripture quotations, unless otherwise noted, are from the *New American Standard Bible*.

of the word of God, that is, the mystery which has been hidden from the past ages and generations, but has now been manifested to His saints, to whom God willed to make known what is the riches of the glory of this mystery among the Gentiles, which is Christ in you, the hope of glory" (Col. 1:27) Also, "So then you are no longer strangers and aliens, but you are fellow citizens with the saints, and are of God's household, having been built on the foundation of the apostles and prophets, Christ Jesus Himself being the corner stone, in whom the whole building, being fitted together, is growing into a holy temple in the Lord, in whom you also are being built together into a dwelling of God in the Spirit" (Eph. 2:19-22). With that being said, let us investigate some infallible scriptures that discuss God's glory!

Chapter Two
GLORY IN THE OLD TESTAMENT

IN THE BOOK OF GENESIS

Let Not My Glory Be United with Their Assembly

"Simeon and Levi are brothers; their swords are implements of violence. Let my soul not enter into their council; let not my glory be united with their assembly; because in their anger they slew men, and in their self-will they lamed oxen. Cursed be their anger, for it is fierce; and their wrath, for it is cruel. I will disperse them in Jacob, and scatter them in Israel" (Ge. 49:5-7).

IN THE BOOK OF EXODUS

In the Morning You Will See the Glory

"Then the Lord said to Moses, 'Behold, I will rain bread from heaven for you; and the people shall go out and gather a day's portion every day, that I may test them, whether or not they will walk in My instruction. On the sixth day, when they prepare what they bring in, it will be twice as much as they gather daily.' So Moses and Aaron said to all the sons of Israel, 'At evening you will know that the Lord has brought you out of the land of Egypt; and in the morning you will see the glory of the Lord, for He hears your grumblings against the Lord; and what are we, that you grumble against us?' Moses said, 'This will happen when the Lord gives you meat to eat in the evening, and bread to the full in the morning; for the Lord hears your grumblings which you grumble against Him. And what are we? Your grumblings are not against us but against the Lord'" (Ex. 16:4-8).

The Glory of the Lord Appeared in the Cloud

"Then Moses said to Aaron, 'Say to all the congregation of the sons of Israel, "Come near before the Lord, for He has heard your grumblings."'" It came about as Aaron spoke to the whole congregation of the sons of Israel, that they looked toward the wilderness, and behold, the glory of the Lord appeared in the cloud. And the Lord spoke to Moses, saying, 'I have heard the grumblings of the sons of Israel; speak to them, saying, "At twilight you shall eat meat, and in the morning you shall be filled with bread; and you shall know that I am the Lord your God"'" (Ex. 16:9-12).

The Glory of the Lord Was Like a Consuming Fire

"Now the Lord said to Moses, 'Come up to Me on the mountain and remain there, and I will give you the stone tablets with the law and the commandment which I have written for their instruction.' So Moses arose with Joshua his servant, and Moses went up to the mountain of God. But to the elders he said, 'Wait here for us until we return to you. And behold, Aaron and Hur are with you; whoever has a legal matter, let him approach them.' Then Moses went up to the mountain, and the cloud covered the mountain. The glory of the Lord rested on Mount Sinai, and the cloud covered it for six days; and on the seventh day He called to Moses from the midst of the cloud. And to the eyes of the sons of Israel the appearance of the glory of the Lord was like a consuming fire on the mountain top. Moses entered the midst of the cloud as he went up to the mountain; and Moses was on the mountain forty days and forty nights" (Ex. 24:12-18).

It Shall Be Consecrated by My Glory

"Now this is what you shall offer on the altar: two one year old lambs each day, continuously. The one lamb you shall offer in the morning and the other lamb you shall offer at twilight; and there shall be one-tenth of an ephah of fine flour mixed with one-fourth of a hin of beaten oil, and one-fourth of a hin of wine for a drink offering with one lamb. The other lamb you shall offer at twilight, and shall offer with it the same grain offering and the same drink offering as in the morning, for a soothing aroma, an offering by fire to the Lord. It shall be a continual burnt offering throughout your generations at the doorway of the tent of meeting before the Lord, where I will meet with you, to speak to you there. I will meet there with the sons of Israel, and it shall be consecrated by My glory. I will consecrate the tent of meeting and the altar; I will also consecrate Aaron and his sons to minister as priests to Me. I will dwell among the sons of Israel and will be their God. They shall know that I am the Lord their God who brought them out of the land of Egypt, that I might dwell among them; I am the Lord their God" (Ex. 29:38-46).

Chapter Two

I Pray Thee, Show Me Thy Glory

"The Lord said to Moses, 'I will also do this thing of which you have spoken; for you have found favor in My sight and I have known you by name.' Then Moses said, 'I pray You, show me Your glory!' And He said, 'I Myself will make all My goodness pass before you, and will proclaim the name of the Lord before you; and I will be gracious to whom I will be gracious, and will show compassion on whom I will show compassion.' But He said, 'You cannot see My face, for no man can see Me and live!' Then the Lord said, 'Behold, there is a place by Me, and you shall stand there on the rock; and it will come about, while My glory is passing by, that I will put you in the cleft of the rock and cover you with My hand until I have passed by. Then I will take My hand away and you shall see My back, but My face shall not be seen'" (Ex. 33:17-23).

The Glory of the Lord Filled the Tabernacle

"Then the cloud covered the tent of meeting, and the glory of the Lord filled the tabernacle. Moses was not able to enter the tent of meeting because the cloud had settled on it, and the glory of the Lord filled the tabernacle. Throughout all their journeys whenever the cloud was taken up from over the tabernacle, the sons of Israel would set out; but if the cloud was not taken up, then they did not set out until the day when it was taken up" (Ex. 40:34-37).

Chapter Two
IN THE BOOK OF LEVITICUS

The Glory of the Lord May Appear to You

"Now it came about on the eighth day that Moses called Aaron and his sons and the elders of Israel; and he said to Aaron, 'Take for yourself a calf, a bull, for a sin offering and a ram for a burnt offering, both without defect, and offer them before the Lord. Then to the sons of Israel you shall speak, saying, "Take a male goat for a sin offering, and a calf and a lamb, both one year old, without defect, for a burnt offering, and an ox and a ram for peace offerings, to sacrifice before the Lord, and a grain offering mixed with oil; for today the Lord will appear to you.'" So they took what Moses had commanded to the front of the tent of meeting, and the whole congregation came near and stood before the Lord. Moses said, 'This is the thing which the Lord has commanded you to do, that the glory of the Lord may appear to you.' Moses then said to Aaron, 'Come near to the altar and offer your sin offering and your burnt offering, that you may make atonement for yourself and for the people; then make the offering for the people, that you may make atonement for them, just as the Lord has commanded'" (Lv. 9:1-7).

The Glory of the Lord Appeared to All the People

"Then Aaron lifted up his hands toward the people and blessed them, and he stepped down after making the sin offering and the burnt offering and the peace offerings. Moses and Aaron went into the tent of meeting. When they came out and blessed the people, the glory of the Lord appeared to all the people. Then fire came out from before the Lord and consumed the burnt offering and the portions of fat on the altar; and when all the people saw it, they shouted and fell on their faces" (Lv. 9:22-24).

IN THE BOOK OF NUMBERS

The Glory of the Lord Appeared in the Tent of Meeting

"Then all the congregation lifted up their voices and cried, and the people wept that night. All the sons of Israel grumbled against Moses and Aaron; and the whole congregation said to them, 'Would that we had died in the land of Egypt! Or would that we had died in this wilderness! Why is the Lord bringing us into this land, to fall by the sword? Our wives and our little ones will become plunder; would it not be better for us to return to Egypt?' So they said to one another, 'Let us appoint a leader and return to Egypt.' Then Moses and Aaron fell on their faces in the presence of all the assembly of the congregation of the sons of Israel. Joshua the son of Nun and Caleb the son of Jephunneh, of those who had spied out the land, tore their clothes; and they spoke to all the congregation of the sons of Israel, saying, 'The land which we passed through to spy out is an exceedingly good land. If the Lord is pleased with us, then He will bring us into this land and give it to us—a land which flows with milk and honey. Only do not rebel against the Lord; and do not fear the people of the land, for they will be our prey. Their protection has been removed from them, and the Lord is with us; do not fear them.' But all the congregation said to stone them with stones. Then the glory of the Lord appeared in the tent of meeting to all the sons of Israel" (Nu. 14:1-10).

All the Earth Will Be Filled with the Glory of the Lord

"So the Lord said, 'I have pardoned them according to your word; but indeed, as I live, all the earth will be filled with the glory of the Lord. Surely all the men who have seen My glory and My signs which I performed in Egypt and in the wilderness, yet have put Me to the test these ten times and have not listened to My voice, shall by no means see the land which I swore to their fathers, nor shall any of those who spurned Me see it. But My servant Caleb, because he has had a different spirit and has followed Me fully, I will bring into the land which he entered, and his descendants shall take possession of it. Now the Amalekites and the Canaanites live in the valleys; turn tomorrow and set out to the wilderness by the way of the Red Sea'" (Nu. 14:20-25).

The Glory of the Lord Appeared To All the Congregation

"Then Moses became very angry and said to the Lord, 'Do not regard their offering! I have not taken a single donkey from them, nor have I done harm to any of them.' Moses said to Korah, 'You and all your company be present before the Lord tomorrow, both you and they along with Aaron. Each of you take his firepan and put incense on it, and each of you bring his censer before the Lord, two hundred and fifty firepans; also you and Aaron shall each bring his firepan.' So they each took his own censer and put fire on it, and laid incense on it; and they stood at the doorway of the tent of meeting, with Moses and Aaron. Thus Korah assembled all the congregation against them at the doorway of the tent of meeting. And the glory of the Lord appeared to all the congregation" (Nu. 16:15-19).

The Cloud Covered It and the Glory of the Lord Appeared

"But on the next day all the congregation of the sons of Israel grumbled against Moses and Aaron, saying, 'You are the ones who have caused the death of the Lord's people.' It came about, however, when the congregation had assembled against Moses and Aaron, that they turned toward the tent of meeting, and behold, the cloud covered it and the glory of the Lord appeared. Then Moses and Aaron came to the front of the tent of meeting, and the Lord spoke to Moses, saying, 'Get away from among this congregation, that I may consume them instantly.' Then they fell on their faces. Moses said to Aaron, 'Take your censer and put in it fire from the altar, and lay incense on it;then bring it quickly to the congregation and make atonement for them, for wrath has gone forth from the Lord, the plague has begun!' Then Aaron took it as Moses had spoken,

Chapter Two

and ran into the midst of the assembly, for behold, the plague had begun among the people. So he put on the incense and made atonement for the people. He took his stand between the dead and the living, so that the plague was checked. But those who died by the plague were 14,700, besides those who died on account of Korah. Then Aaron returned to Moses at the doorway of the tent of meeting, for the plague had been checked" (Nu. 16:41-50).

Moses and Aaron Fell on Their Faces and the Glory Appeared

"There was no water for the congregation, and they assembled themselves against Moses and Aaron. The people thus contended with Moses and spoke, saying, 'If only we had perished when our brothers perished before the Lord! Why then have you brought the Lord's assembly into this wilderness, for us and our beasts to die here? Why have you made us come up from Egypt, to bring us in to this wretched place? It is not a place of grain or figs or vines or pomegranates, nor is there water to drink.' Then Moses and Aaron came in from the presence of the assembly to the doorway of the tent of meeting and fell on their faces. Then the glory of the Lord appeared to them; and the LORD spoke to Moses, saying, 'Take the rod; and you and your brother Aaron assemble the congregation and speak to the rock before their eyes, that it may yield its water. You shall thus bring forth water for them out of the rock and let the congregation and their beasts drink'" (Nu. 20:2-8).

Chapter Two
IN THE BOOK OF DEUTERONOMY

God Has Shown Us His Glory and His Greatness

"These words the Lord spoke to all your assembly at the mountain from the midst of the fire, of the cloud and of the thick gloom, with a great voice, and He added no more. He wrote them on two tablets of stone and gave them to me. And when you heard the voice from the midst of the darkness, while the mountain was burning with fire, you came near to me, all the heads of your tribes and your elders. You said, 'Behold, the Lord our God has shown us His glory and His greatness, and we have heard His voice from the midst of the fire; we have seen today that God speaks with man, yet he lives. 'Now then why should we die? For this great fire will consume us; if we hear the voice of the Lord our God any longer, then we will die. For who is there of all flesh who has heard the voice of the living God speaking from the midst of the fire, as we have, and lived? Go near and hear all that the Lord our God says; then speak to us all that the Lord our God speaks to you, and we will hear and do it'" (Dt. 5:22-27).

IN THE BOOK OF JOSHUA

My Son, I Implore You, Give Glory to the Lord

"So Joshua arose early in the morning and brought Israel near by tribes, and the tribe of Judah was taken. He brought the family of Judah near, and he took the family of the Zerahites; and he brought the family of the Zerahites near man by man, and Zabdi was taken. He brought his household near man by man; and Achan, son of Carmi, son of Zabdi, son of Zerah, from the tribe of Judah, was taken. Then Joshua said to Achan, 'My son, I implore you, give glory to the Lord, the God of Israel, and give praise to Him; and tell me now what you have done. Do not hide it from me.' So Achan answered Joshua and said, 'Truly, I have sinned against the Lord, the God of Israel, and this is what I did: when I saw among the spoil a beautiful mantle from Shinar and two hundred shekels of silver and a bar of gold fifty shekels in weight, then I coveted them and took them; and behold, they are concealed in the earth inside my tent with the silver underneath it'" (Jos. 7:16-21).

IN THE BOOK OF 1 SAMUEL

The Glory Has Departed from Israel

"Now his daughter-in-law, Phinehas's wife, was pregnant and about to give birth; and when she heard the news that the ark of God was taken and that her father-in-law and her husband had died, she kneeled down and gave birth, for her pains came upon her. And about the time of her death the women who stood by her said to her, 'Do not be afraid, for you have given birth to a son.' But she did not answer or pay attention. And she called the boy Ichabod, saying, 'The glory has departed from Israel,' because the ark of God was taken and because of her father-in-law and her husband. She said, 'The glory has departed from Israel, for the ark of God was taken'" (1Sa. 4:19-22).

Give Glory to the God of Israel; Perhaps He Will Ease His Hand from You

"Now the ark of the Lord had been in the country of the Philistines seven months. And the Philistines called for the priests and the diviners, saying, 'What shall we do with the ark of the Lord? Tell us how we shall send it to its place.' They said, 'If you send away the ark of the God of Israel, do not send it empty; but you shall surely return to Him a guilt offering. Then you will be healed and it will be known to you why His hand is not removed from you.' Then they said, 'What shall be the guilt offering which we shall return to Him?' And they said, 'Five golden tumors and five golden mice according to the number of the lords of the Philistines, for one plague was on all of you and on your lords. So you shall make likenesses of your tumors and likenesses of your mice that ravage the land, and you shall give glory to the God of Israel; perhaps He will ease His hand from you, your gods, and your land. Why then do you harden your hearts as the Egyptians and Pharaoh hardened their hearts? When He had severely dealt with them, did they not allow the people to go, and they departed? Now therefore, take and prepare a new cart and two milch cows on which there has never been a yoke; and hitch the cows to the cart and take their calves home, away from them. Take the ark of the Lord and place it on the cart; and put the articles of gold which you return to Him as a guilt offering in a box by its side.

Chapter Two

Then send it away that it may go. Watch, if it goes up by the way of its own territory to Beth-shemesh, then He has done us this great evil. But if not, then we will know that it was not His hand that struck us; it happened to us by chance'" (1Sa. 6:1-9).

The Glory of Israel Will Not Lie or Change His Mind

"Then Saul said to Samuel, 'I have sinned; I have indeed transgressed the command of the Lord and your words, because I feared the people and listened to their voice. Now therefore, please pardon my sin and return with me, that I may worship the Lord.' But Samuel said to Saul, 'I will not return with you; for you have rejected the word of the Lord, and the Lord has rejected you from being king over Israel.' As Samuel turned to go, Saul seized the edge of his robe, and it tore. So Samuel said to him, 'The Lord has torn the kingdom of Israel from you today and has given it to your neighbor, who is better than you. Also the Glory of Israel will not lie or change His mind; for He is not a man that He should change His mind.' Then he said, 'I have sinned; but please honor me now before the elders of my people and before Israel, and go back with me, that I may worship the Lord your God.' So Samuel went back following Saul, and Saul worshiped the Lord" (1Sa. 15:24-31).

Chapter Two

IN THE BOOK OF 1 KINGS

The Priests Could Not Stand to Minister Because of the Glory

"Then Solomon assembled the elders of Israel and all the heads of the tribes, the leaders of the fathers' households of the sons of Israel, to King Solomon in Jerusalem, to bring up the ark of the covenant of the Lord from the city of David, which is Zion. All the men of Israel assembled themselves to King Solomon at the feast, in the month Ethanim, which is the seventh month. Then all the elders of Israel came, and the priests took up the ark. They brought up the ark of the Lord and the tent of meeting and all the holy utensils, which were in the tent, and the priests and the Levites brought them up. And King Solomon and all the congregation of Israel, who were assembled to him, were with him before the ark, sacrificing so many sheep and oxen they could not be counted or numbered. Then the priests brought the ark of the covenant of the Lord to its place, into the inner sanctuary of the house, to the most holy place, under the wings of the cherubim. For the cherubim spread their wings over the place of the ark, and the cherubim made a covering over the ark and its poles from above. But the poles were so long that the ends of the poles could be seen from the holy place before the inner sanctuary, but they could not be seen outside; they are there to this day. There was nothing in the ark except the two tablets of stone which Moses put there at Horeb, where the Lord made a covenant with the sons of Israel, when they came out of the land of Egypt. It happened that

Chapter Two

when the priests came from the holy place, the cloud filled the house of the Lord, so that the priests could not stand to minister because of the cloud, for the glory of the Lord filled the house of the Lord" (1Ki. 8:1-11).

IN THE BOOK OF 1 CHRONICLES

Glory in His Holy Name

"Then on that day David first assigned Asaph and his relatives to give thanks to the Lord. Oh give thanks to the Lord, call upon His name; Make known His deeds among the peoples. Sing to Him, sing praises to Him; Speak of all His wonders. Glory in His holy name; Let the heart of those who seek the Lord be glad. Seek the Lord and His strength; Seek His face continually. Remember His wonderful deeds which He has done, His marvels and the judgments from His mouth, O seed of Israel His servant, Sons of Jacob, His chosen ones! He is the Lord our God; His judgments are in all the earth. Remember His covenant forever, The word which He commanded to a thousand generations, The covenant which He made with Abraham, And His oath to Isaac. He also confirmed it to Jacob for a statute, To Israel as an everlasting covenant, Saying, 'To you I will give the land of Canaan, As the portion of your inheritance.' When they were only a few in number, Very few, and strangers in it, And they wandered about from nation to nation, And from one kingdom to another people, He permitted no man to oppress them, And He reproved kings for their sakes, saying, 'Do not touch My anointed ones,

And do My prophets no harm.' Sing to the Lord, all the earth; Proclaim good tidings of His salvation from day to day. Tell of His glory among the nations, His wonderful deeds among all the peoples. For great is the Lord, and greatly to be praised; He also is to be feared above all gods. For all the gods of the peoples are idols, But the Lord made the heavens. Splendor and majesty are before Him, Strength and joy are in His place. Ascribe to the Lord, O families of the peoples, Ascribe to the Lord glory and strength. Ascribe to the Lord the glory due His name; Bring an offering, and come before Him; Worship the Lord in holy array. Tremble before Him, all the earth; Indeed, the world is firmly established, it will not be moved. Let the heavens be glad, and let the earth rejoice; And let them say among the nations, "The Lord reigns." Let the sea roar, and all it contains; Let the field exult, and all that is in it. Then the trees of the forest will sing for joy before the Lord; For He is coming to judge the earth. O give thanks to the Lord, for He is good; For His lovingkindness is everlasting. Then say, 'Save us, O God of our salvation, And gather us and deliver us from the nations, To give thanks to Your holy name, And glory in Your praise.' Blessed be the Lord, the God of Israel, From everlasting even to everlasting. Then all the people said, 'Amen,' and praised the Lord" (1Ch. 16:7-36).

Thine, O Lord, Is the Greatness and the Power and the Glory and the Victory and the Majesty

"So David blessed the Lord in the sight of all the assembly; and David said, 'Blessed are You, O

Chapter Two

Lord God of Israel our father, forever and ever. Yours, O Lord, is the greatness and the power and the glory and the victory and the majesty, indeed everything that is in the heavens and the earth; Yours is the dominion, O Lord, and You exalt Yourself as head over all. Both riches and honor come from You, and You rule over all, and in Your hand is power and might; and it lies in Your hand to make great and to strengthen everyone. Now therefore, our God, we thank You, and praise Your glorious name'" (1Ch. 29:10-13).

IN THE BOOK OF 2 CHRONICLES

The Glory of the Lord Filled the House of God

"When the priests came forth from the holy place (for all the priests who were present had sanctified themselves, without regard to divisions), and all the Levitical singers, Asaph, Heman, Jeduthun, and their sons and kinsmen, clothed in fine linen, with cymbals, harps and lyres, standing east of the altar, and with them one hundred and twenty priests blowing trumpets in unison when the trumpeters and the singers were to make themselves heard with one voice to praise and to glorify the Lord, and when they lifted up their voice accompanied by trumpets and cymbals and instruments of music, and when they praised the Lord saying, 'He indeed is good for His lovingkindness is everlasting,' then the house, the house of the Lord, was filled with a cloud, so that the priests could not stand to minister because of the cloud, for the glory of the Lord filled the house of God" (2Ch. 5:11-14).

Fire Consumed the Burnt Offering and the Sacrifices; and the Glory Filled the House

"Now when Solomon had finished praying, fire came down from heaven and consumed the burnt offering and the sacrifices, and the glory of the Lord filled the house. The priests could not enter into the house of the Lord because the glory of the Lord filled the Lord's house. All the sons of Israel, seeing the fire come down and the glory of the Lord upon the house, bowed down on the pavement with their faces to the ground, and they worshiped and gave praise to the Lord, saying, 'Truly He is good, truly His lovingkindness is everlasting'" (2Ch. 7:1-3).

IN THE BOOK OF PSALMS

O Lord, Art a Shield about Me, My Glory, and the One Who Lifts My Head

"But You, O Lord, are a shield about me, My glory, and the One who lifts my head. I was crying to the Lord with my voice, And He answered me from His holy mountain. I lay down and slept; I awoke, for the Lord sustains me. I will not be afraid of ten thousands of people Who have set themselves against me round about" (Ps. 3:3-6).

Chapter Two

The Heavens Are Telling of the Glory of God

"The heavens are telling of the glory of God; And their expanse is declaring the work of His hands. Day to day pours forth speech, And night to night reveals knowledge. There is no speech, nor are there words; Their voice is not heard. Their line has gone out through all the earth, And their utterances to the end of the world. In them He has placed a tent for the sun, Which is as a bridegroom coming out of his chamber; It rejoices as a strong man to run his course. Its rising is from one end of the heavens, And its circuit to the other end of them; And there is nothing hidden from its heat" (Ps. 19:1-6).

His Glory Is Great through Thy Salvation

"O Lord, in Your strength the king will be glad, And in Your salvation how greatly he will rejoice! You have given him his heart's desire, And You have not withheld the request of his lips. For You meet him with the blessings of good things; You set a crown of fine gold on his head. He asked life of You, You gave it to him, Length of days forever and ever. His glory is great through Your salvation, Splendor and majesty You place upon him. For You make him most blessed forever; You make him joyful with gladness in Your presence" (Ps. 21:1-6).

That the King of Glory May Come In

"Lift up your heads, O gates, And be lifted up, O ancient doors, That the King of glory may come in! Who is the King of glory? The Lord strong and mighty, The Lord mighty in battle. Lift up your heads, O gates, And lift them up, O ancient doors, That the King of glory may come in! Who is this King of glory? The Lord of hosts, He is the King of glory" (Ps. 24:7-10).

The Place Where Thy Glory Dwells

"O Lord, I love the habitation of Your house And the place where Your glory dwells. Do not take my soul away along with sinners, Nor my life with men of bloodshed, In whose hands is a wicked scheme, And whose right hand is full of bribes. But as for me, I shall walk in my integrity; Redeem me, and be gracious to me. My foot stands on a level place; In the congregations I shall bless the Lord" (Ps. 26:8-12).

Ascribe to the Lord Glory and Strength

"Ascribe to the Lord, O sons of the mighty, Ascribe to the Lord glory and strength. Ascribe to the Lord the glory due to His name; Worship the Lord in holy array" (Ps. 29:1-2).

The God of Glory Thunders

"The voice of the Lord is upon the waters; The God of glory thunders, The Lord is over many waters. The voice of the Lord is powerful, The voice of the Lord is majestic. The voice of the Lord breaks the cedars; Yes, the Lord breaks in pieces the cedars of Lebanon. He makes Lebanon skip like a calf, And Sirion like a young wild ox. The voice of the Lord hews out flames of fire. The voice of the Lord shakes the wilderness; The Lord shakes the wilderness of Kadesh. The voice of the Lord makes the deer to calve And strips the forests bare; And in His temple everything says, 'Glory!'" (Ps. 29:3-9).

O God; Let Thy Glory Be Above All the Earth

"My soul is among lions; I must lie among those who breathe forth fire, Even the sons of men, whose teeth are spears and arrows And their tongue a sharp sword. Be exalted above the heavens, O God; Let Your glory be above all the earth. They have prepared a net for my steps; My soul is bowed down; They dug a pit before me; They themselves have fallen into the midst of it" (Ps. 57:4-6).

Awake, My Glory; Awake, Harp and Lyre

"My heart is steadfast, O God, my heart is steadfast; I will sing, yes, I will sing praises! Awake, my glory! Awake, harp and lyre! I will awaken the dawn. I will give thanks to You, O Lord, among the peoples; I will sing praises to You among the nations.   For Your lovingkindness is great to the heavens And Your truth to the clouds. Be exalted above the heavens, O God; Let Your glory be above all the earth" (Ps. 57:7-11).

On God My Salvation and My Glory Rest

"My soul, wait in silence for God only, For my hope is from Him. He only is my rock and my salvation, My stronghold; I shall not be shaken. On

Chapter Two

God my salvation and my glory rest; The rock of my strength, my refuge is in God. Trust in Him at all times, O people; Pour out your heart before Him; God is a refuge for us" (Ps. 62:5-8).

To See Thy Power and Thy Glory

"O God, You are my God; I shall seek You earnestly; My soul thirsts for You, my flesh yearns for You, In a dry and weary land where there is no water. Thus I have seen You in the sanctuary, To see Your power and Your glory. Because Your lovingkindness is better than life, My lips will praise You. So I will bless You as long as I live; I will lift up my hands in Your name. My soul is satisfied as with marrow and fatness, And my mouth offers praises with joyful lips" (Ps. 63:1-5).

Everyone Who Swears by Him Will Glory

"But those who seek my life to destroy it, Will go into the depths of the earth. They will be delivered over to the power of the sword; They will be a prey for foxes. But the king will rejoice in God; Everyone who swears by Him will glory, For the mouths of those who speak lies will be stopped" (Ps. 63:9-11).

All the Upright in Heart Will Glory

"But God will shoot at them with an arrow; Suddenly they will be wounded. So they will make him stumble; Their own tongue is against them; All who see them will shake the head. Then all men will fear, And they will declare the work of God, And will consider what He has done. The righteous man will be glad in the Lord and will take refuge in Him; And all the upright in heart will glory" (Ps. 64:7-10).

Sing the Glory of His Name; Make His Praise Glorious

"Shout joyfully to God, all the earth; Sing the glory of His name; Make His praise glorious. Say to God, "How awesome are Your works! Because of the greatness of Your power Your enemies will give feigned obedience to You. All the earth will worship You, And will sing praises to You; They will sing praises to Your name" (Ps. 66:1-4).

My Mouth Is Filled with Thy Praise, and with Thy Glory All Day Long

"I have become a marvel to many, For You are my strong refuge. My mouth is filled with Your praise And with Your glory all day long. Do not cast me off in the time of old age; Do not forsake me when my strength fails. For my enemies have spoken against me; And those who watch for my life have consulted together, Saying, 'God has forsaken him; Pursue and seize him, for there is no one to deliver'" (Ps. 71:7-11).

May the Whole Earth Be Filled with His Glory

"Blessed be the Lord God, the God of Israel, Who alone works wonders. And blessed be His glorious name forever; And may the whole earth be filled with His glory. Amen, and Amen" (Ps. 72:18-19).

Guide Me, and Afterward Receive Me to Glory

"If I had said, 'I will speak thus,' Behold, I would have betrayed the generation of Your children. When I pondered to understand this, It was troublesome in my sight Until I came into the sanctuary of God; Then I perceived their end. Surely You set them in slippery places; You cast them down to destruction. How they are destroyed in a moment! They are utterly swept away by sudden terrors! Like a dream when one awakes, O Lord, when aroused, You will despise their form. When my heart was embittered And I was pierced within, Then I was senseless and ignorant; I was like a beast before You. Nevertheless I am continually with You; You have taken hold of my right hand. With Your counsel You will guide me, And afterward receive me to glory" (Ps. 73:15-24).

His Glory into the Hand of the Adversary

"So He brought them to His holy land, To this hill country which His right hand had gained. He also drove out the nations before them And apportioned them for an inheritance by measurement, And made the tribes of Israel dwell in their tents. Yet they tempted and rebelled against the Most High God And did not keep His testimonies, But turned back and acted treacherously like their fathers; They turned aside like a treacherous bow. For they provoked Him with their high places And aroused His jealousy with their graven images. When God heard, He was filled with wrath And greatly abhorred Israel; So that He abandoned the dwelling place at Shiloh, The tent which He had pitched among men, And gave up His strength to captivity And His glory into the hand of the adversary. He also delivered His people to the sword, And was filled with wrath at His inheritance. Fire devoured His young men, And His virgins had no wedding songs. His priests fell by the sword, And His widows could not weep" (Ps. 78:54-64).

Help Us, O God of Our Salvation, for the Glory of Thy Name

"Do not remember the iniquities of our forefathers against us; Let Your compassion come quickly to meet us, For we are brought very low. Help us, O God of our salvation, for the glory of Your name; And deliver us and forgive our sins for Your name's sake. Why should the nations say, 'Where is their God?' Let there be known among the nations in our sight, Vengeance for the blood of Your servants which has been shed. Let the groaning of the prisoner come before You; According to the greatness of Your power preserve those who are doomed to die. And return to our neighbors sevenfold into their bosom The reproach with which they have reproached You, O Lord. So we Your people and the sheep of Your pasture Will give thanks to You forever; To all generations we will tell of Your praise" (Ps. 79:8-13).

Chapter Two

The Lord Gives Grace and Glory

"O Lord God of hosts, hear my prayer; Give ear, O God of Jacob! Behold our shield, O God, And look upon the face of Your anointed. For a day in Your courts is better than a thousand outside. I would rather stand at the threshold of the house of my God Than dwell in the tents of wickedness. For the Lord God is a sun and shield; The Lord gives grace and glory; No good thing does He withhold from those who walk uprightly. O Lord of hosts, How blessed is the man who trusts in You" (Ps. 84:8-121)!

That Glory May Dwell in our Land

"I will hear what God the Lord will say; For He will speak peace to His people, to His godly ones; But let them not turn back to folly. Surely His salvation is near to those who fear Him, That glory may dwell in our land. Lovingkindness and truth have met together; Righteousness and peace have kissed each other. Truth springs from the earth, And righteousness looks down from heaven. Indeed, the Lord will give what is good, And our land will yield its produce. Righteousness will go before Him And will make His footsteps into a way" (Ps. 85:8-13).

For Thou Art the Glory of Their Strength

"The heavens are Yours, the earth also is Yours; The world and all it contains, You have founded them. The north and the south, You have created them; Tabor and Hermon shout for joy at

Chapter Two

Your name. You have a strong arm; Your hand is mighty, Your right hand is exalted. Righteousness and justice are the foundation of Your throne; Lovingkindness and truth go before You. How blessed are the people who know the joyful sound! O Lord, they walk in the light of Your countenance. In Your name they rejoice all the day, And by Your righteousness they are exalted. For You are the glory of their strength, And by Your favor our horn is exalted. For our shield belongs to the Lord, And our king to the Holy One of Israel" (Ps. 89:11-18).

Tell of His Glory Among the Nations

"Sing to the Lord a new song; Sing to the Lord, all the earth. Sing to the Lord, bless His name; Proclaim good tidings of His salvation from day to day. Tell of His glory among the nations, His wonderful deeds among all the peoples. For great is the Lord and greatly to be praised; He is to be feared above all gods. For all the gods of the peoples are idols, But the Lord made the heavens. Splendor and majesty are before Him, Strength and beauty are in His sanctuary" (Ps. 96:1-6).

Ascribe to the Lord Glory and Strength

"Ascribe to the Lord, O families of the peoples, Ascribe to the Lord glory and strength. Ascribe to the Lord the glory of His name; Bring an offering and come into His courts. Worship the Lord in holy attire; Tremble before Him, all the earth. Say among the nations, 'The Lord reigns; Indeed, the world is firmly established, it will not be moved; He will judge the peoples with equity'" (Ps. 96:7-10).

All the Peoples Have Seen His Glory

"The Lord reigns, let the earth rejoice; Let the many islands be glad. Clouds and thick darkness surround Him; Righteousness and justice are the foundation of His throne. Fire goes before Him And burns up His adversaries round about. His lightnings lit up the world; The earth saw and trembled. The mountains melted like wax at the presence of the Lord, At the presence of the Lord of the whole earth. The heavens declare His righteousness, And all the peoples have seen His glory" (Ps. 97:1-6).

Nations Will Fear and All the Kings of the Earth Thy Glory

"But You, O Lord, abide forever, And Your name to all generations. You will arise and have compassion on Zion; For it is time to be gracious to her, For the appointed time has come. Surely Your servants find pleasure in her stones And feel pity for her dust. So the nations will fear the name of the Lord And all the kings of the earth Your glory. For the Lord has built up Zion; He has appeared in His glory. He has regarded the prayer of the destitute And has not despised their prayer" (Ps. 102:12-17).

Chapter Two

Let the Glory of the Lord Endure Forever

"Let the glory of the Lord endure forever; Let the Lord be glad in His works; He looks at the earth, and it trembles; He touches the mountains, and they smoke. I will sing to the Lord as long as I live; I will sing praise to my God while I have my being. Let my meditation be pleasing to Him; As for me, I shall be glad in the Lord. Let sinners be consumed from the earth And let the wicked be no more. Bless the Lord, O my soul. Praise the Lord" (Ps. 104:31-36)!

Glory in His Holy Name

"Oh give thanks to the Lord, call upon His name; Make known His deeds among the peoples. Sing to Him, sing praises to Him; Speak of all His wonders. Glory in His holy name; Let the heart of those who seek the Lord be glad. Seek the Lord and His strength; Seek His face continually. Remember His wonders which He has done, His marvels and the judgments uttered by His mouth, O seed of Abraham, His servant, O sons of Jacob, His chosen ones! He is the Lord our God; His judgments are in all the earth" (Ps. 105:1-7).

That I May Glory with Thine Inheritance

"Remember me, O Lord, in Your favor toward Your people; Visit me with Your salvation, That I may see the prosperity of Your chosen ones, That I may rejoice in the gladness of Your nation, That I may glory with Your inheritance" (Ps. 106:4-5).

Chapter Two

To Give Thanks to Thy Holy Name, and Glory in Thy Praise

"Save us, O Lord our God, And gather us from among the nations, To give thanks to Your holy name And glory in Your praise. Blessed be the Lord, the God of Israel, From everlasting even to everlasting. And let all the people say, 'Amen.' Praise the Lord" (Ps. 106:47-48)!

Be Exalted, O God, Above the Heavens, and Thy Glory Above All the Earth

"My heart is steadfast, O God; I will sing, I will sing praises, even with my soul. Awake, harp and lyre; I will awaken the dawn! I will give thanks to You, O Lord, among the peoples, And I will sing praises to You among the nations. For Your lovingkindness is great above the heavens, And Your truth reaches to the skies. Be exalted, O God, above the heavens, And Your glory above all the earth. That Your beloved may be delivered, Save with Your right hand, and answer me" (Ps. 108:1-6)!

His Glory Is Above the Heavens

"Praise the Lord! Praise, O servants of the Lord, Praise the name of the Lord. Blessed be the name of the Lord From this time forth and forever. From the rising of the sun to its setting The name of the Lord is to be praised. The Lord is high above all nations; His glory is above the heavens" (Ps. 113:1-4).

Chapter Two

To Thy Name Give Glory

"Not to us, O Lord, not to us, But to Your name give glory Because of Your lovingkindness, because of Your truth. Why should the nations say, 'Where, now, is their God?' But our God is in the heavens; He does whatever He pleases. Their idols are silver and gold, The work of man's hands. They have mouths, but they cannot speak; They have eyes, but they cannot see; They have ears, but they cannot hear; They have noses, but they cannot smell; They have hands, but they cannot feel; They have feet, but they cannot walk; They cannot make a sound with their throat. Those who make them will become like them, Everyone who trusts in them" (Ps. 115:1-8).

For Great Is the Glory of the Lord

"All the kings of the earth will give thanks to You, O Lord, When they have heard the words of Your mouth. And they will sing of the ways of the Lord, For great is the glory of the Lord. For though the Lord is exalted, Yet He regards the lowly, But the haughty He knows from afar" (Ps. 138:4-6).

They Shall Speak of the Glory of Thy Kingdom, and Talk of Thy Power

"The Lord is gracious and merciful; Slow to anger and great in lovingkindness. The Lord is good to all, And His mercies are over all His works. All Your works shall give thanks to You, O Lord, And Your godly ones shall bless You. They shall speak of the glory of Your kingdom And talk of Your power; To make known to the sons of men Your mighty acts And the glory of the majesty of Your kingdom. Your kingdom is an everlasting kingdom, And Your dominion endures throughout all generations" (Ps. 145:8-13).

His Name Alone Is Exalted; His Glory Is Above Earth and Heaven

"Let them praise the name of the Lord, For His name alone is exalted; His glory is above earth and heaven. And He has lifted up a horn for His people, Praise for all His godly ones; Even for the sons of Israel, a people near to Him. Praise the Lord" (Ps. 148:13-14).

Let the Godly Ones Exult in Glory

"Let the godly ones exult in glory; Let them sing for joy on their beds. Let the high praises of God be in their mouth, and a two-edged sword in their hand, to execute vengeance on the nations And punishment on the peoples, to bind their kings with chains And their nobles with fetters of iron, to execute on them the judgment written; this is an honor for all His godly ones. Praise the Lord" (Ps. 149:5-9).

Chapter Two
IN THE BOOK OF PROVERBS

In a Multitude of People is a King's Glory

"In a multitude of people is a king's glory, But in the dearth of people is a prince's ruin" (Pr. 14:28).

The Glory of Kings Is to Search Out a Matter

"It is the glory of God to conceal a matter, But the glory of kings is to search out a matter. As the heavens for height and the earth for depth, So the heart of kings is unsearchable. Take away the dross from the silver, And there comes out a vessel for the smith; Take away the wicked before the king, And his throne will be established in righteousness. Do not claim honor in the presence of the king, And do not stand in the place of great men; For it is better that it be said to you, 'Come up here,' Than for you to be placed lower in the presence of the prince, Whom your eyes have seen" (Pr. 25:2-7).

IN THE BOOK OF ISAIAH

Over All the Glory Will Be a Canopy.

"In that day the Branch of the Lord will be beautiful and glorious, and the fruit of the earth will be the pride and the adornment of the survivors of Israel. It will come about that he who is left in Zion and remains in Jerusalem will be called holy — everyone who is recorded for life in Jerusalem. When the Lord has washed away the filth of the daughters of Zion and purged the bloodshed of Jerusalem from her midst, by the spirit of judgment and the spirit of burning, then the LORD will create over the whole area of Mount Zion and over her assemblies a cloud by day, even smoke, and the brightness of a flaming fire by night; for over all the glory will be a canopy. There will be a shelter to give shade from the heat by day, and refuge and protection from the storm and the rain" (Is. 4:2-6).

Holy, Holy, Holy, Is the Lord of Hosts, the Whole Earth is Full of His Glory

"In the year of King Uzziah's death I saw the Lord sitting on a throne, lofty and exalted, with the train of His robe filling the temple. Seraphim stood above Him, each having six wings: with two he covered his face, and with two he covered his feet, and with two he flew. And one called out to another and said, 'Holy, Holy, Holy, is the Lord of hosts, The whole earth is full of His glory.' And the foundations of the thresholds trembled at the voice of him who called out, while the temple was filling with smoke. Then I said, 'Woe is me, for I am ruined! Because I am a man of unclean lips, And I live among a people of unclean lips; For my eyes have seen the King, the Lord of hosts'" (Is. 6:1-5).

Under His Glory a Fire Will Be Kindled Like a Burning Flame

"Is the axe to boast itself over the one who chops with it? Is the saw to exalt itself over the one who wields it? That would be like a club wielding those who lift it, Or like a rod lifting him who is not wood. Therefore the Lord, the God of hosts, will send a wasting disease among his stout warriors; And under his glory a fire will be kindled like a burning flame. And the light of Israel will become a fire and his Holy One a flame, And it will burn and devour his thorns and his briars in a single day. And He will destroy the glory of his forest and of his fruitful garden, both soul and body, And it will be as when a sick man wastes away. And the rest of the trees of his forest will be so small in number That a child could write them down" (Is. 10:15-19).

From the Ends of the Earth We Hear Songs, Glory to the Righteous One

"The new wine mourns, The vine decays, All the merry-hearted sigh. The gaiety of tambourines ceases, The noise of revelers stops, The gaiety of the harp ceases. They do not drink wine with song; Strong drink is bitter to those who drink it. The city of chaos is broken down; Every house is shut up so that none may enter. There is an outcry in the streets concerning the wine; All joy turns to gloom. The gaiety of the earth is banished. Desolation is left in the city And the gate is battered to ruins. For thus it will be in the midst of the earth among the peoples, As the shaking of an olive tree, As the gleanings when the grape harvest is over. They raise their voices, they shout for joy; They cry out from the west concerning the majesty of the Lord. Therefore glorify the Lord in the east, The name of the Lord, the God of Israel, In the coastlands of the sea. From the ends of the earth we hear songs, 'Glory to the

Chapter Two

Righteous One,' But I say, 'Woe to me! Woe to me! Alas for me! The treacherous deal treacherously, And the treacherous deal very treacherously.' Terror and pit and snare Confront you, O inhabitant of the earth. Then it will be that he who flees the report of disaster will fall into the pit, And he who climbs out of the pit will be caught in the snare; For the windows above are opened, and the foundations of the earth shake. The earth is broken asunder, The earth is split through, The earth is shaken violently. The earth reels to and fro like a drunkard And it totters like a shack, For its transgression is heavy upon it, And it will fall, never to rise again. So it will happen in that day, That the Lord will punish the host of heaven on high, And the kings of the earth on earth. They will be gathered together Like prisoners in the dungeon, And will be confined in prison; And after many days they will be punished. Then the moon will be abashed and the sun ashamed, For the Lord of hosts will reign on Mount Zion and in Jerusalem, And His glory will be before His elders" (Is. 24:7-23).

They Will See the Glory of the Lord, the Majesty of Our God

"The wilderness and the desert will be glad, And the Arabah will rejoice and blossom; Like the crocus It will blossom profusely And rejoice with rejoicing and shout of joy. The glory of Lebanon will be given to it, The majesty of Carmel and Sharon. They will see the glory of the Lord, The majesty of our God. Encourage the exhausted, and strengthen the feeble. Say to those with anxious heart, 'Take courage, fear not. Behold, your God will come with vengeance; The recompense of God will come, But He will save you.' Then the eyes of the blind will be opened And the ears of the deaf will be unstopped. Then the lame will leap like a deer, And the tongue of the mute will shout for joy. For waters will break forth in the wilderness And streams in the Arabah. The scorched land will become a pool And the thirsty ground springs of water; In the haunt of jackals, its resting place, Grass becomes reeds and rushes. A highway will be there, a roadway, And it will be called the Highway of Holiness. The unclean will not travel on it, But it will be for him who walks that way, And fools will not wander on it. No lion will be there, Nor will any vicious beast go up on it; These will not be found there. But the redeemed will walk there, And the ransomed of the Lord will return And come with joyful shouting to Zion, With everlasting joy upon their heads. They will find gladness and joy, And sorrow and sighing will flee away" (Is. 35:1-10).

The Glory of the Lord Will Be Revealed

"A voice is calling, 'Clear the way for the Lord in the wilderness; Make smooth in the desert a highway for our God. Let every valley be lifted up, And every mountain and hill be made low; And let the rough ground become a plain, And the rugged terrain a broad valley; Then the glory of the Lord will be revealed, And all flesh will see it together; For the mouth of the Lord has spoken.' A voice says, 'Call out.' Then he answered, 'What shall I call out?' All flesh is grass, and all its loveliness is like the flower of the field. The grass withers, the flower fades, When the breath of the Lord blows upon it; Surely the people are grass. The grass withers, the flower fades, But the word of our God stands forever" (Is. 40:3-8).

You Will Glory in the Holy One of Israel

"The coastlands have seen and are afraid; The ends of the earth tremble; They have drawn near and have come. Each one helps his neighbor And says to his brother, 'Be strong!' So the craftsman encourages the smelter, And he who smooths metal with the hammer encourages him who beats the anvil, Saying of the soldering, 'It is good'; And he fastens it with nails, So that it will not totter. 'But you, Israel, My servant, Jacob whom I have chosen, Descendant of Abraham My friend, You whom I have taken from the ends of the earth, And called from its remotest parts And said to you, "You are My servant, I have chosen you and not rejected you. Do not fear, for I am with you; Do not anxiously look about you, for I am your God. I will strengthen you, surely I will help you, Surely I will uphold you with My righteous right hand." Behold, all those who are angered at you will be shamed and dishonored; Those who contend with you will be as nothing and will perish. You will seek those who quarrel with you, but will not find them, Those who war with you will be as nothing and non-existent. For I am the Lord your God, who upholds your right hand, Who says to you, "Do not fear, I will help you." Do not fear, you worm Jacob, you men of Israel; I will help you,' declares the Lord, 'and your Redeemer is the

Holy One of Israel. Behold, I have made you a new, sharp threshing sledge with double edges; You will thresh the mountains and pulverize them, And will make the hills like chaff. You will winnow them, and the wind will carry them away, And the storm will scatter them; But you will rejoice in the Lord, You will glory in the Holy One of Israel'" (Is. 41:5-16).

I Am the Lord, that Is My Name; I Will Not Give My Glory to Another

"Thus says God the Lord, Who created the heavens and stretched them out, Who spread out the earth and its offspring, Who gives breath to the people on it And spirit to those who walk in it, I am the Lord, I have called you in righteousness, I will also hold you by the hand and watch over you, And I will appoint you as a covenant to the people, As a light to the nations, To open blind eyes, To bring out prisoners from the dungeon And those who dwell in darkness from the prison. I am the Lord, that is My name; I will not give My glory to another, Nor My praise to graven images. Behold, the former things have come to pass, Now I declare new things; Before they spring forth I proclaim them to you" (Is. 42:5-9).

Let Them Give Glory to the Lord, and Declare His Praise in the Coastlands

"Sing to the Lord a new song, Sing His praise from the end of the earth! You who go down to the sea, and all that is in it. You islands, and those who dwell on them. Let the wilderness and its cities lift up their voices, The settlements where Kedar inhabits. Let the inhabitants of Sela sing aloud, Let them shout for joy from the tops of the mountains. Let them give glory to the Lord And declare His praise in the coastlands.   The Lord will go forth like a warrior, He will arouse His zeal like a man of war. He will utter a shout, yes, He will raise a war cry. He will prevail against His enemies" (Is. 42:10-13).

Whom I Have Created for My Glory

"But now, thus says the Lord, your Creator, O Jacob, And He who formed you, O Israel, 'Do not fear, for I have redeemed you; I have called you by name; you are Mine! When you pass through the waters, I will be with you; And through the rivers, they will not overflow you. When you walk through the fire, you will not be scorched, Nor will the flame burn you. For I am the Lord your God, The Holy One of Israel, your Savior; I have given Egypt as your ransom, Cush and Seba in your place. Since you are precious in My sight, Since you are honored and I love you, I will give other men in your place and other peoples in exchange for your life. Do not fear, for I am with you; I will bring your offspring from the east, And gather you from the west. I will say to the north, "Give them up!" And to the south, "Do not hold them back." Bring My sons from afar And My daughters from the ends of the earth, Everyone who is called by My name, And whom I have created for My glory, Whom I have formed, even whom I have made'" (Is. 43:1-7).

Chapter Two

The Lord Has Redeemed Jacob and in Israel He Shows Forth His Glory

"Remember these things, O Jacob, And Israel, for you are My servant; I have formed you, you are My servant, O Israel, you will not be forgotten by Me. I have wiped out your transgressions like a thick cloud And your sins like a heavy mist. Return to Me, for I have redeemed you. Shout for joy, O heavens, for the Lord has done it! Shout joyfully, you lower parts of the earth; Break forth into a shout of joy, you mountains, O forest, and every tree in it; For the Lord has redeemed Jacob And in Israel He shows forth His glory" (Is. 44:21-23).

In the Lord All the Offspring of Israel Will Be Justified, and Will Glory

"Gather yourselves and come; Draw near together, you fugitives of the nations; They have no knowledge, Who carry about their wooden idol And pray to a god who cannot save. Declare and set forth your case; Indeed, let them consult together. Who has announced this from of old? Who has long since declared it? Is it not I, the Lord? And there is no other God besides Me, A righteous God and a Savior; There is none except Me. Turn to Me and be saved, all the ends of the earth; For I am God, and there is no other. I have sworn by Myself, The word has gone forth from My mouth in righteousness And will not turn back, That to Me every knee will bow, every tongue will swear allegiance. They will say of Me, 'Only in the Lord are righteousness and strength.' Men will come to Him, And all who were angry at Him will be put to shame. In the Lord all the offspring of Israel Will be justified and will glory" (Is. 45:20-25).

I Will Grant Salvation in Zion, and My Glory for Israel

"Listen to Me, you stubborn-minded, Who are far from righteousness. I bring near My righteousness, it is not far off; And My salvation will not delay. And I will grant salvation in Zion, And My glory for Israel" (Is. 46:12-13).

My Glory I Will Not Give to Another

"Hear this, O house of Jacob, who are named Israel And who came forth from the loins of Judah, Who swear by the name of the Lord And invoke the God of Israel, But not in truth nor in righteousness. For they call themselves after the holy city And lean on the God of Israel; The Lord of hosts is His name. I declared the former things long ago And they went forth from My mouth, and I proclaimed them. Suddenly I acted, and they came to pass. Because I know that you are obstinate, And your neck is an iron sinew And your forehead bronze, Therefore I declared them to you long ago, Before they took place I proclaimed them to you, So that you would not say, 'My idol has done them, And my graven image and my molten image have commanded them.' You have heard; look at all this. And you, will you not declare it? I proclaim to you new things from this time, Even hidden things which you have not known. They are created now and not long ago;

Chapter Two

And before today you have not heard them, So that you will not say, 'Behold, I knew them.' You have not heard, you have not known. Even from long ago your ear has not been open, Because I knew that you would deal very treacherously; And you have been called a rebel from birth. For the sake of My name I delay My wrath, And for My praise I restrain it for you, In order not to cut you off. Behold, I have refined you, but not as silver; I have tested you in the furnace of affliction. For My own sake, for My own sake, I will act; For how can My name be profaned? And My glory I will not give to another" (Is. 48:1-11).

You Are My Servant, Israel, In Whom I Will Show My Glory

"Listen to Me, O islands, And pay attention, you peoples from afar. The Lord called Me from the womb; From the body of My mother He named Me. He has made My mouth like a sharp sword, In the shadow of His hand He has concealed Me; And He has also made Me a select arrow, He has hidden Me in His quiver. He said to Me, 'You are My Servant, Israel, In Whom I will show My glory.' But I said, 'I have toiled in vain, I have spent My strength for nothing and vanity; Yet surely the justice due to Me is with the Lord, And My reward with My God'" (Is. 49:1-4).

The Glory of the Lord Will Be Your Rear Guard

"Cry loudly, do not hold back; Raise your voice like a trumpet, And declare to My people their transgression And to the house of Jacob their sins. Yet they seek Me day by day and delight to know My ways, As a nation that has done righteousness And has not forsaken the ordinance of their God. They ask Me for just decisions, They delight in the nearness of God. Why have we fasted and You do not see? Why have we humbled ourselves and You do not notice?' Behold, on the day of your fast you find your desire, And drive hard all your workers. Behold, you fast for contention and strife and to strike with a wicked fist. You do not fast like you do today to make your voice heard on high. Is it a fast like this which I choose, a day for a man to humble himself? Is it for bowing one's head like a reed And for spreading out sackcloth and ashes as a bed? Will you call this a fast, even an acceptable day to the Lord? Is this not the fast which I choose, To loosen the bonds of wickedness, To undo the bands of the yoke, And to let the oppressed go free And break every yoke? Is it not to divide your bread with the hungry And bring the homeless poor into the house; When you see the naked, to cover him; And not to hide yourself from your own flesh? Then your light will break out like the dawn, And your recovery will speedily spring forth; And your righteousness will go before you; The glory of the Lord will be your rear guard. Then you will call, and the Lord will answer; You will cry, and He will say, 'Here I am.' If you remove the yoke from your midst, The pointing of the finger and speaking wickedness, And if you give yourself to the hungry And satisfy the desire of the afflicted, Then your light will rise in darkness And your gloom will become like midday. And the Lord will continually guide you, And satisfy your desire in scorched places, And give strength to your bones; And you will be like a watered garden, And like a spring of water whose waters do not fail. Those from among you will rebuild the ancient ruins; You will raise up the age-old foundations; And you will be called the repairer of the breach, The restorer of the streets in which to dwell" (Is. 58:1-12).

They Will Fear the Name of the Lord from the West and His Glory from the Rising of the Sun

"'Therefore justice is far from us, And righteousness does not overtake us; We hope for light, but behold, darkness, For brightness, but we walk in gloom. We grope along the wall like blind men, We grope like those who have no eyes; We stumble at midday as in the twilight, Among those who are vigorous we are like dead men. All of us growl like bears, And moan sadly like doves; We hope for justice, but there is none, For salvation, but it is far from us.   For our transgressions are multiplied before You, And our sins testify against us; For our transgressions are with us, And we know our iniquities: Transgressing and denying the Lord, And turning away from our God, Speaking oppression and revolt, Conceiving in and uttering from the heart lying words. Justice is turned back, And righteousness stands far away; For truth has stumbled in the street, And uprightness cannot enter. Yes, truth is lacking; And he who turns aside from evil makes himself a prey. Now the Lord saw, And it was displeasing in His sight that there was no justice. And He saw that there was no man, And was astonished that there was no one to intercede; Then His own arm brought salvation to Him, And His righteousness upheld Him. He put on righteousness like a breastplate, And a helmet of salvation on His head; And He put on garments of vengeance for clothing And wrapped Himself with zeal as a mantle. According to their deeds, so He will repay, Wrath to His adversaries, recompense to His enemies; To the coastlands He will make recompense. So they will fear the name of the Lord from the west And His glory from the rising of the sun, For He will come like a rushing stream Which the wind of the Lord drives. A Redeemer will come to Zion, And to those who turn from transgression in Jacob,' declares the Lord" (Is. 59:9-20).

Arise, Shine; for your Light Has Come, and the Glory of the Lord Has Risen Upon You

"Arise, shine; for your light has come, And the glory of the Lord has risen upon you. For behold, darkness will cover the earth And deep darkness the peoples; But the Lord will rise upon you And His glory will appear upon you. Nations will come to your light, And kings to the brightness of your rising" (Is. 60:1-3).

The Glory of Lebanon Will Come to You, The Juniper, the Box Tree, and the Cypress Together

"Foreigners will build up your walls, And their kings will minister to you; For in My wrath I struck you, And in My favor I have had compassion on you. Your gates will be open continually; They will not be closed day or night, So that men may bring to you the wealth of the nations, With their kings led in procession. For the nation and the kingdom which will not serve you will perish, And the nations will be utterly ruined. The glory of Lebanon will come to you, The juniper, the box tree and the cypress together, To beautify the place of My sanctuary; And I shall make the place of My feet glorious. The sons of those who afflicted you will come bowing to you, And all those who despised you will bow themselves at the soles of your feet; And they will call you the city of the Lord, The Zion of the Holy One of Israel" (Is. 60:10-14).

You Will Have the Lord for an Everlasting Light, and Your God for Your Glory

"Whereas you have been forsaken and hated With no one passing through, I will make you an everlasting pride, A joy from generation to generation. You will also suck the milk of nations And suck the breast of kings; Then you will know that I, the Lord, am your Savior And your Redeemer, the Mighty One of Jacob. Instead of bronze I will bring gold, And instead of iron I will bring silver, And instead of wood, bronze, And instead of stones, iron. And I will make peace your administrators And righteousness your overseers. Violence will not be heard again in your land, Nor devastation or destruction within your borders; But you will call your walls salvation, and your gates praise. No longer will you have the sun for light by day, Nor for brightness will the moon give you light; But you will have the Lord for an everlasting light, And your

Chapter Two

God for your glory. Your sun will no longer set, Nor
will your moon wane; For you will have the Lord for
an everlasting light, And the days of your mourning
will be over. Then all your people will be righteous;
They will possess the land forever, The branch of My
planting, The work of My hands, That I may be
glorified. The smallest one will become a clan, And
the least one a mighty nation. I, the Lord, will hasten
it in its time" (Is. 60:15-22).

Nations and Tongues Shall Come and See My Glory

"'For I know their works and their thoughts;
the time is coming to gather all nations and tongues.
And they shall come and see My glory. I will set a
sign among them and will send survivors from them
to the nations: Tarshish, Put, Lud, Meshech, Rosh,
Tubal and Javan, to the distant coastlands that have
neither heard My fame nor seen My glory. And they
will declare My glory among the nations. Then they
shall bring all your brethren from all the nations as a
grain offering to the Lord, on horses, in chariots, in
litters, on mules and on camels, to My holy
mountain Jerusalem,' says the Lord, 'just as the sons
of Israel bring their grain offering in a clean vessel to
the house of the Lord. I will also take some of them
for priests and for Levites,' says the Lord. 'For just as
the new heavens and the new earth Which I make
will endure before Me,' declares the Lord, 'So your
offspring and your name will endure. And it shall be
from new moon to new moon And from sabbath to
sabbath, All mankind will come to bow down before
Me,' says the Lord. Then they will go forth and look

Chapter Two

On the corpses of the men Who have transgressed against Me. For their worm will not die And their fire will not be quenched; And they will be an abhorrence to all mankind" (Is. 66:18-24).

IN THE BOOK OF JEREMIAH

In Him They Will Glory

"'If you will return, O Israel,' declares the Lord, 'Then you should return to Me. And if you will put away your detested things from My presence, And will not waver, And you will swear, "As the Lord lives," In truth, in justice and in righteousness; Then the nations will bless themselves in Him, And in Him they will glory'" (Jer. 4:1-2).

A People, for Renown, for Praise, and for Glory; but They Did Not Listen

"Then the word of the Lord came to me, saying, 'Thus says the Lord, "Just so will I destroy the pride of Judah and the great pride of Jerusalem. This wicked people, who refuse to listen to My words, who walk in the stubbornness of their hearts and have gone after other gods to serve them and to bow down to them, let them be just like this waistband which is totally worthless. For as the waistband clings to the waist of a man, so I made the whole household of Israel and the whole household of Judah cling to Me," declares the Lord, "that they might be for Me a people, for renown, for praise and for glory; but they did not listen"'" (Jer. 13:8-11).

Chapter Two

Give glory to the Lord, Before Your Feet Stumble on the Dusky Mountains

"Listen and give heed, do not be haughty, For the Lord has spoken. Give glory to the Lord your God, Before He brings darkness And before your feet stumble On the dusky mountains, And while you are hoping for light He makes it into deep darkness, And turns it into gloom. But if you will not listen to it, My soul will sob in secret for such pride; And my eyes will bitterly weep And flow down with tears, Because the flock of the Lord has been taken captive. Say to the king and the queen mother, 'Take a lowly seat, For your beautiful crown Has come down from your head.' The cities of the Negev have been locked up, And there is no one to open them; All Judah has been carried into exile, Wholly carried into exile" (Jer. 13:15-19).

Do Not Disgrace the Throne of Thy Glory

"Have You completely rejected Judah? Or have You loathed Zion? Why have You stricken us so that we are beyond healing? We waited for peace, but nothing good came; And for a time of healing, but behold, terror! We know our wickedness, O Lord, The iniquity of our fathers, for we have sinned against You. Do not despise us, for Your own name's sake; Do not disgrace the throne of Your glory; Remember and do not annul Your covenant with us. Are there any among the idols of the nations who give rain? Or can the heavens grant showers? Is it not You, O Lord our God? Therefore we hope in

You, For You are the one who has done all these things" (Jer. 14:19-22).

It Shall Be to Me a Name of Joy, Praise, and Glory Before all the Nations of the Earth

"Then the word of the Lord came to Jeremiah the second time, while he was still confined in the court of the guard, saying, 'Thus says the Lord who made the earth, the Lord who formed it to establish it, the Lord is His name, "Call to Me and I will answer you, and I will tell you great and mighty things, which you do not know." For thus says the Lord God of Israel concerning the houses of this city, and concerning the houses of the kings of Judah which are broken down to make a defense against the siege ramps and against the sword, "While they are coming to fight with the Chaldeans and to fill them with the corpses of men whom I have slain in My anger and in My wrath, and I have hidden My face from this city because of all their wickedness: Behold, I will bring to it health and healing, and I will heal them; and I will reveal to them an abundance of peace and truth. I will restore the fortunes of Judah and the fortunes of Israel and will rebuild them as they were at first. I will cleanse them from all their iniquity by which they have sinned against Me, and I will pardon all their iniquities by which they have sinned against Me and by which they have transgressed against Me. It will be to Me a name of joy, praise and glory before all the nations of the earth which will hear of all the good that I do for them, and they will fear and tremble because of all the good and all the peace that I make for it"""" (Jer. 33:1-9).

IN THE BOOK OF EZEKIEL

The Likeness of the Glory

"Now above the expanse that was over their heads there was something resembling a throne, like lapis lazuli in appearance; and on that which resembled a throne, high up, was a figure with the appearance of a man. Then I noticed from the appearance of His loins and upward something like glowing metal that looked like fire all around within it, and from the appearance of His loins and downward I saw something like fire; and there was a radiance around Him. As the appearance of the rainbow in the clouds on a rainy day, so was the appearance of the surrounding radiance. Such was the appearance of the likeness of the glory of the Lord. And when I saw it, I fell on my face and heard a voice speaking" (Eze. 1:26-28).

Blessed Be the Glory of the Lord in His Place

"Then the Spirit lifted me up, and I heard a great rumbling sound behind me, 'Blessed be the glory of the Lord in His place.' And I heard the sound of the wings of the living beings touching one another and the sound of the wheels beside them, even a great rumbling sound. So the Spirit lifted me up and took me away; and I went embittered in the rage of my spirit, and the hand of the Lord was strong on me. Then I came to the exiles who lived beside the river Chebar at Tel-abib, and I sat there seven days where they were living, causing consternation among them" (Eze. 3:12-15).

Like the Glory Which I Saw by the River Chebar, and I Fell on My Face

"The hand of the Lord was on me there, and He said to me, 'Get up, go out to the plain, and there I will speak to you.' So I got up and went out to the plain; and behold, the glory of the Lord was standing there, like the glory which I saw by the river Chebar, and I fell on my face. The Spirit then entered me and made me stand on my feet, and He spoke with me and said to me, 'Go, shut yourself up in your house. As for you, son of man, they will put ropes on you and bind you with them so that you cannot go out among them. Moreover, I will make your tongue stick to the roof of your mouth so that you will be mute and cannot be a man who rebukes them, for they are a rebellious house. But when I speak to you, I will open your mouth and you will say to them, "Thus says the Lord God." He who hears, let him hear; and he who refuses, let him refuse; for they are a rebellious house'" (Eze. 3:22-27).

Behold, the Glory of the God of Israel Was There

"It came about in the sixth year, on the fifth day of the sixth month, as I was sitting in my house with the elders of Judah sitting before me, that the hand of the Lord God fell on me there. Then I looked, and behold, a likeness as the appearance of a man; from His loins and downward there was the appearance of fire, and from His loins and upward the appearance of brightness, like the appearance of glowing metal. He stretched out the form of a hand and caught me by a lock of my head; and the Spirit lifted me up between earth and heaven and brought me in the visions of God to Jerusalem, to the entrance of the north gate of the inner court, where the seat of the idol of jealousy, which provokes to jealousy, was located. And behold, the glory of the God of Israel was there, like the appearance which I saw in the plain" (Eze. 8:1-4).

The Glory of the God of Israel Went up from the Cherub

"Then the glory of the God of Israel went up from the cherub on which it had been, to the threshold of the temple. And He called to the man clothed in linen at whose loins was the writing case. The Lord said to him, 'Go through the midst of the city, even through the midst of Jerusalem, and put a mark on the foreheads of the men who sigh and groan over all the abominations which are being committed in its midst.' But to the others He said in my hearing, 'Go through the city after him and strike; do not let your eye have pity and do not spare. Utterly slay old men, young men, maidens, little children, and women, but do not touch any man on whom is the mark; and you shall start from My sanctuary.' So they started with the elders who were before the temple. And He said to them, 'Defile the temple and fill the courts with the slain. Go out!' Thus they went out and struck down the people in the city. As they were striking the people and I alone was left, I fell on my face and cried out saying, 'Alas, Lord God! Are You destroying the whole remnant of Israel by pouring out Your wrath on Jerusalem?"' (Eze. 9:3-8).

The Glory of the Lord Went up from the Cherub to the Threshold of the Temple

"Now the cherubim were standing on the right side of the temple when the man entered, and the cloud filled the inner court. Then the glory of the Lord went up from the cherub to the threshold of the temple, and the temple was filled with the cloud and the court was filled with the brightness of the glory of the Lord. Moreover, the sound of the wings of the cherubim was heard as far as the outer court, like the voice of God Almighty when He speaks" (Eze. 10:3-5).

The Glory Stood Over the Cherubim

"Then the glory of the Lord departed from the threshold of the temple and stood over the cherubim. When the cherubim departed, they lifted their wings and rose up from the earth in my sight with the wheels beside them; and they stood still at the entrance of the east gate of the Lord's house, and the glory of the God of Israel hovered over them" (Eze. 10:18-19).

Chapter Two

The Glory of the God of Israel Hovered

"Then the cherubim lifted up their wings with the wheels beside them, and the glory of the God of Israel hovered over them. The glory of the Lord went up from the midst of the city and stood over the mountain which is east of the city. And the Spirit lifted me up and brought me in a vision by the Spirit of God to the exiles in Chaldea. So the vision that I had seen left me. Then I told the exiles all the things that the Lord had shown me" (Eze. 11:22-25).

I Shall Set My Glory Among the Nations

"And I will set My glory among the nations; and all the nations will see My judgment which I have executed and My hand which I have laid on them. And the house of Israel will know that I am the Lord their God from that day onward. The nations will know that the house of Israel went into exile for their iniquity because they acted treacherously against Me, and I hid My face from them; so I gave them into the hand of their adversaries, and all of them fell by the sword. According to their uncleanness and according to their transgressions I dealt with them, and I hid My face from them" (Eze. 39:21-24).

The Glory of the God of Israel Was Coming from the Way of the East

"Then he led me to the gate, the gate facing toward the east; and behold, the glory of the God of Israel was coming from the way of the east. And His voice was like the sound of many waters; and the earth shone with His glory. And it was like the appearance of the vision which I saw, like the vision which I saw when He came to destroy the city. And the visions were like the vision which I saw by the river Chebar; and I fell on my face. And the glory of the Lord came into the house by the way of the gate facing toward the east. And the Spirit lifted me up and brought me into the inner court; and behold, the glory of the Lord filled the house" (Eze. 43:1-5).

The Glory of the Lord Filled the House and I Fell on My Face

"Then He brought me by way of the north gate to the front of the house; and I looked, and behold, the glory of the Lord filled the house of the Lord, and I fell on my face. The Lord said to me, 'Son of man, mark well, see with your eyes and hear with your ears all that I say to you concerning all the statutes of the house of the Lord and concerning all its laws; and mark well the entrance of the house, with all exits of the sanctuary. You shall say to the rebellious ones, to the house of Israel, "Thus says the Lord God, 'Enough of all your abominations, O house of Israel, when you brought in foreigners, uncircumcised in heart and uncircumcised in flesh, to be in My sanctuary to profane it, even My house, when you offered My food, the fat and the blood; for they made My covenant void — this in addition to all your abominations. And you have not kept charge of My holy things yourselves, but you have set foreigners to keep charge of My sanctuary"""" (Eze. 44:4-8).

Chapter Two

IN THE BOOK OF DANIEL

The God of Heaven Has Given the Kingdom, the Power, the Strength, and the Glory

"This was the dream; now we will tell its interpretation before the king. 'You, O king, are the king of kings, to whom the God of heaven has given the kingdom, the power, the strength and the glory; and wherever the sons of men dwell, or the beasts of the field, or the birds of the sky, He has given them into your hand and has caused you to rule over them all. You are the head of gold. After you there will arise another kingdom inferior to you, then another third kingdom of bronze, which will rule over all the earth. Then there will be a fourth kingdom as strong as iron; inasmuch as iron crushes and shatters all things, so, like iron that breaks in pieces, it will crush and break all these in pieces. In that you saw the feet and toes, partly of potter's clay and partly of iron, it will be a divided kingdom; but it will have in it the toughness of iron, inasmuch as you saw the iron mixed with common clay. As the toes of the feet were partly of iron and partly of pottery, so some of the kingdom will be strong and part of it will be brittle. And in that you saw the iron mixed with common clay, they will combine with one another in the seed of men; but they will not adhere to one another, even as iron does not combine with pottery. In the days of those kings the God of heaven will set up a kingdom which will never be destroyed, and that kingdom will not be left for another people; it will crush and put an end to all these kingdoms, but it will itself endure forever. Inasmuch as you saw that a stone was cut out of the mountain without hands and that it crushed the iron, the bronze, the clay, the silver and the gold, the great God has made knowr to the king what will take place in the future; so the dream is true and its interpretation is trustworthy'" (Da. 2:36-45).

To Him Was Given Dominion, Glory and a Kingdom

"I kept looking in the night visions, And behold, with the clouds of heaven One like a Son of Man was coming, And He came up to the Ancient of Days And was presented before Him. And to Him was given dominion, Glory and a kingdom, That all the peoples, nations and men of every language Might serve Him. His dominion is an everlasting dominion Which will not pass away; And His kingdom is one Which will not be destroyed" (Da. 7:13-14).

IN THE BOOK OF HABAKKUK

The Earth Will Be Filled with the Knowledge of the Glory of the Lord

"Woe to him who builds a city with bloodshed And founds a town with violence! Is it not indeed from the Lord of hosts That peoples toil for fire, And nations grow weary for nothing? For the earth will be filled With the knowledge of the glory of the Lord, As the waters cover the sea" (Hab. 2:12-14).

Chapter Two

IN THE BOOK OF HAGGAI

I Will Shake All the Nations; and They Will Come with the Wealth of All Nations

"On the twenty-first of the seventh month, the word of the Lord came by Haggai the prophet saying, Speak now to Zerubbabel the son of Shealtiel, governor of Judah, and to Joshua the son of Jehozadak, the high priest, and to the remnant of the people saying, 'Who is left among you who saw this temple in its former glory? And how do you see it now? Does it not seem to you like nothing in comparison? But now take courage, Zerubbabel,' declares the Lord, 'take courage also, Joshua son of Jehozadak, the high priest, and all you people of the land take courage,' declares the Lord, 'and work; for I am with you,' declares the Lord of hosts. As for the promise which I made you when you came out of Egypt, My Spirit is abiding in your midst; do not fear!' For thus says the Lord of hosts, 'Once more in a little while, I am going to shake the heavens and the earth, the sea also and the dry land. I will shake all the nations; and they will come with the wealth of all nations, and I will fill this house with glory,' says the Lord of hosts. 'The silver is Mine and the gold is Mine,' declares the Lord of hosts. 'The latter glory of this house will be greater than the former,' says the Lord of hosts, 'and in this place I will give peace,' declares the Lord of hosts." (Hag. 2:1-9).

Chapter Two

IN THE BOOK OF ZECHARIAH

I Will Be the Glory in Her Midst

"Then I lifted up my eyes and looked, and behold, there was a man with a measuring line in his hand. So I said, 'Where are you going?' And he said to me, 'To measure Jerusalem, to see how wide it is and how long it is.' And behold, the angel who was speaking with me was going out, and another angel was coming out to meet him, and said to him, 'Run, speak to that young man, saying, "Jerusalem will be inhabited without walls because of the multitude of men and cattle within it. For I," declares the Lord, "will be a wall of fire around her, and I will be the glory in her midst"'" (Zec. 2:1-5).

After Glory He Has Sent Me Against the Nations

"'Ho there! Flee from the land of the north,' declares the Lord, 'for I have dispersed you as the four winds of the heavens,' declares the Lord. 'Ho, Zion! Escape, you who are living with the daughter of Babylon.' For thus says the Lord of hosts, 'After glory He has sent me against the nations which plunder you, for he who touches you, touches the apple of His eye. For behold, I will wave My hand over them so that they will be plunder for their slaves. Then you will know that the Lord of hosts has sent Me. Sing for joy and be glad, O daughter of Zion; for behold I am coming and I will dwell in your midst,' declares the Lord. 'Many nations will join themselves to the Lord in that day and will become My people. Then I will dwell in your midst,

and you will know that the Lord of hosts has sent
Me to you. The Lord will possess Judah as His
portion in the holy land, and will again choose
Jerusalem'" (Zec. 2:6-12).

Chapter Three

GLORY IN THE NEW TESTAMENT

IN THE BOOK OF MATTHEW

For Thine Is the Kingdom, and the Power, and the Glory, Forever

"Pray, then, in this way: 'Our Father who is in heaven, Hallowed be Your name. Your kingdom come. Your will be done, On earth as it is in heaven. Give us this day our daily bread. And forgive us our debts, as we also have forgiven our debtors. And do not lead us into temptation, but deliver us from evil. For Yours is the kingdom and the power and the glory forever. Amen. For if you forgive others for their transgressions, your heavenly Father will also forgive you. But if you do not forgive others, then your Father will not forgive your transgressions'" (Mt. 6:9-15).

The Son of Man Is Going to Come in the Glory of His Father with His Angels

"Then Jesus said to His disciples, 'If anyone wishes to come after Me, he must deny himself, and take up his cross and follow Me. For whoever wishes to save his life will lose it; but whoever loses his life for My sake will find it. For what will it profit a man if he gains the whole world and forfeits his soul? Or what will a man give in exchange for his soul? For the Son of Man is going to come in the glory of His Father with His angels, and WILL THEN REPAY EVERY MAN ACCORDING TO HIS DEEDS'" (Mt. 16:24-27).

Chapter Three

They Will See the Son of Man Coming on the Clouds of the Sky with Power and Great Glory

"But immediately after the tribulation of those days THE SUN WILL BE DARKENED, AND THE MOON WILL NOT GIVE ITS LIGHT, AND THE STARS WILL FALL from the sky, and the powers of the heavens will be shaken. And then the sign of the Son of Man will appear in the sky, and then all the tribes of the earth will mourn, and they will see the SON OF MAN COMING ON THE CLOUDS OF THE SKY with power and great glory. And He will send forth His angels with A GREAT TRUMPET and THEY WILL GATHER TOGETHER His elect from the four winds, from one end of the sky to the other" (Mt. 24:29-31).

IN THE BOOK OF MARK

The Son of Man Will Also Be Ashamed of Him When He Comes in the Glory of His Father

"And He summoned the crowd with His disciples, and said to them, 'If anyone wishes to come after Me, he must deny himself, and take up his cross and follow Me. For whoever wishes to save his life will lose it, but whoever loses his life for My sake and the gospel's will save it. For what does it profit a man to gain the whole world, and forfeit his soul? For what will a man give in exchange for his soul? For whoever is ashamed of Me and My words in this adulterous and sinful generation, the Son of Man will also be ashamed of him when He comes in the glory of His Father with the holy angels'" (Mk. 8:34-38).

Chapter Three

Grant that We May Sit in Your Glory

"James and John, the two sons of Zebedee, came up to Jesus, saying, 'Teacher, we want You to do for us whatever we ask of You.' And He said to them, 'What do you want Me to do for you?' They said to Him, 'Grant that we may sit, one on Your right and one on Your left, in Your glory.' But Jesus said to them, 'You do not know what you are asking. Are you able to drink the cup that I drink, or to be baptized with the baptism with which I am baptized?' They said to Him, 'We are able.' And Jesus said to them, 'The cup that I drink you shall drink; and you shall be baptized with the baptism with which I am baptized. But to sit on My right or on My left, this is not Mine to give; but it is for those for whom it has been prepared'" (Mk. 10:35-40).

They Will See the Son of Man Coming in Clouds with Great Power and Glory

"But in those days, after that tribulation, THE SUN WILL BE DARKENED AND THE MOON WILL NOT GIVE ITS LIGHT, AND THE STARS WILL BE FALLING from heaven, and the powers that are in the heavens will be shaken. Then they will see THE SON OF MAN COMING IN CLOUDS with great power and glory. And then He will send forth the angels, and will gather together His elect from the four winds, from the farthest end of the earth to the farthest end of heaven" (Mk. 13:24-27).

Chapter Three

IN THE BOOK OF LUKE

An Angel of the Lord Suddenly Stood Before Them, and the Glory of the Lord Shone Around Them

"In the same region there were some shepherds staying out in the fields and keeping watch over their flock by night. And an angel of the Lord suddenly stood before them, and the glory of the Lord shone around them; and they were terribly frightened. But the angel said to them, 'Do not be afraid; for behold, I bring you good news of great joy which will be for all the people; for today in the city of David there has been born for you a Savior, who is Christ the Lord. This will be a sign for you: you will find a baby wrapped in cloths and lying in a manger.' And suddenly there appeared with the angel a multitude of the heavenly host praising God and saying, 'Glory to God in the highest, And on earth peace among men with whom He is pleased'" (Lk. 2:8-14).

The Glory of Thy People Israel

"And there was a man in Jerusalem whose name was Simeon; and this man was righteous and devout, looking for the consolation of Israel; and the Holy Spirit was upon him. And it had been revealed to him by the Holy Spirit that he would not see death before he had seen the Lord's Christ. And he came in the Spirit into the temple; and when the parents brought in the child Jesus, to carry out for Him the custom of the Law, then he took Him into his arms, and blessed God, and said, 'Now Lord, You are releasing Your bond-servant to depart in peace, According to Your word; For my eyes have seen Your salvation, Which You have prepared in the presence of all peoples, A LIGHT OF REVELATION TO THE GENTILES, And the glory of Your people Israel"' (Lk. 2:25-32).

When He Comes in His Glory, and the Glory of the Father

"And it happened that while He was praying alone, the disciples were with Him, and He questioned them, saying, 'Who do the people say that I am?' They answered and said, 'John the Baptist, and others say Elijah; but others, that one of the prophets of old has risen again.' And He said to them, 'But who do you say that I am?' And Peter answered and said. 'The Christ of God.' But He warned them and instructed them not to tell this to anyone, saying, 'The Son of Man must suffer many things and be rejected by the elders and chief priests and scribes, and be killed and be raised up on the third day.' And He was saying to them all, 'If anyone wishes to come after Me, he must deny himself, and take up his cross daily and follow Me. For whoever wishes to save his life will lose it, but whoever loses his life for My sake, he is the one who will save it. For what is a man profited if he gains the whole world, and loses or forfeits himself? For whoever is ashamed of Me and My words, the Son of Man will be ashamed of him when He comes in His glory, and the glory of the Father and of the holy angels. But I say to you truthfully, there are some of those standing here who will not taste death until they see the kingdom of God"' (Lk. 9:18-27).

Chapter Three

Appearing in Glory

"Some eight days after these sayings, He took along Peter and John and James, and went up on the mountain to pray. And while He was praying, the appearance of His face became different, and His clothing became white and gleaming. And behold, two men were talking with Him; and they were Moses and Elijah, who, appearing in glory, were speaking of His departure which He was about to accomplish at Jerusalem. Now Peter and his companions had been overcome with sleep; but when they were fully awake, they saw His glory and the two men standing with Him. And as these were leaving Him, Peter said to Jesus, 'Master, it is good for us to be here; let us make three tabernacles: one for You, and one for Moses, and one for Elijah'—not realizing what he was saying. While he was saying this, a cloud formed and began to overshadow them; and they were afraid as they entered the cloud. Then a voice came out of the cloud, saying, 'This is My Son, My Chosen One; listen to Him!' And when the voice had spoken, Jesus was found alone. And they kept silent, and reported to no one in those days any of the things which they had seen" (Lk. 9:28-36).

Was No One Found Who Turned Back to Give Glory to God

"While He was on the way to Jerusalem, He was passing between Samaria and Galilee. As He entered a village, ten leprous men who stood at a distance met Him; and they raised their voices, saying, 'Jesus, Master, have mercy on us!' When He saw them, He said to them, 'Go and show yourselves to the priests.' And as they were going, they were cleansed. Now one of them, when he saw that he had been healed, turned back, glorifying God with a loud voice, and he fell on his face at His feet, giving thanks to Him. And he was a Samaritan. Then Jesus answered and said, 'Were there not ten cleansed? But the nine — where are they? Was no one found who returned to give glory to God, except this foreigner?' And He said to him, 'Stand up and go; your faith has made you well''' (Lk. 17:11-19).

Peace in Heaven and Glory in the Highest

"When He approached Bethphage and Bethany, near the mount that is called Olivet, He sent two of the disciples, saying, 'Go into the village ahead of you; there, as you enter, you will find a colt tied on which no one yet has ever sat; untie it and bring it here. If anyone asks you, "Why are you untying it?" you shall say, "The Lord has need of it.'" So those who were sent went away and found it just as He had told them. As they were untying the colt, its owners said to them, 'Why are you untying the colt?' They said, 'The Lord has need of it.' They brought it to Jesus, and they threw their coats on the colt and put Jesus on it. As He was going, they were spreading their coats on the road. As soon as He was approaching, near the descent of the Mount of Olives, the whole crowd of the disciples began to praise God joyfully with a loud voice for all the miracles which they had seen, shouting: 'BLESSED IS THE KING WHO COMES IN THE NAME OF THE LORD; Peace in heaven and glory in the highest!' Some of the Pharisees in the crowd said to Him, 'Teacher, rebuke Your disciples.' But Jesus answered, 'I tell you, if these become silent, the stones will cry out''' (Lk. 19:29-40)!

Chapter Three

With Power and Great Glory

"There will be signs in sun and moon and stars, and on the earth dismay among nations, in perplexity at the roaring of the sea and the waves, men fainting from fear and the expectation of the things which are coming upon the world; for the powers of the heavens will be shaken. Then they will see THE SON OF MAN COMING IN A CLOUD with power and great glory. But when these things begin to take place, straighten up and lift up your heads, because your redemption is drawing near" (Lk. 21:25-28).

To Enter into His Glory

"And behold, two of them were going that very day to a village named Emmaus, which was about seven miles from Jerusalem. And they were talking with each other about all these things which had taken place. While they were talking and discussing, Jesus Himself approached and began traveling with them. But their eyes were prevented from recognizing Him. And He said to them, 'What are these words that you are exchanging with one another as you are walking?' And they stood still, looking sad. One of them, named Cleopas, answered and said to Him, 'Are You the only one visiting Jerusalem and unaware of the things which have happened here in these days?' And He said to them, 'What things?' And they said to Him, 'The things about Jesus the Nazarene, who was a prophet mighty in deed and word in the sight of God and all the people, and how the chief priests and our rulers delivered Him to the sentence of death, and crucified Him. But we were hoping that it was He who was going to redeem

Israel. Indeed, besides all this, it is the third day since these things happened. But also some women among us amazed us. When they were at the tomb early in the morning, and did not find His body, they came, saying that they had also seen a vision of angels who said that He was alive. Some of those who were with us went to the tomb and found it just exactly as the women also had said; but Him they did not see.' And He said to them, 'O foolish men and slow of heart to believe in all that the prophets have spoken! Was it not necessary for the Christ to suffer these things and to enter into His glory?' Then beginning with Moses and with all the prophets, He explained to them the things concerning Himself in all the Scriptures" (Lk. 24:13-27).

IN THE BOOK OF JOHN

We Beheld His Glory, Glory as of the Only Begotten from the Father, Full of Grace and Truth

"And the Word became flesh, and dwelt among us, and we saw His glory, glory as of the only begotten from the Father, full of grace and truth. John testified about Him and cried out, saying, 'This was He of whom I said, "He who comes after me has a higher rank than I, for He existed before me."' For of His fullness we have all received, and grace upon grace. For the Law was given through Moses; grace and truth were realized through Jesus Christ. No one has seen God at any time; the only begotten God who is in the bosom of the Father, He has explained Him" (Jn. 1:14-18).

Chapter Three

Jesus Manifested His Glory, and His Disciples Believed in Him

"On the third day there was a wedding in Cana of Galilee, and the mother of Jesus was there; and both Jesus and His disciples were invited to the wedding. When the wine ran out, the mother of Jesus *said to Him, 'They have no wine.' And Jesus said to her, 'Woman, what does that have to do with us? My hour has not yet come.' His mother said to the servants, 'Whatever He says to you, do it.' Now there were six stone waterpots set there for the Jewish custom of purification, containing twenty or thirty gallons each. Jesus said to them, 'Fill the waterpots with water.' So they filled them up to the brim. And He said to them, 'Draw some out now and take it to the headwaiter.' So they took it to him. When the headwaiter tasted the water which had become wine, and did not know where it came from (but the servants who had drawn the water knew), the headwaiter called the bridegroom, and said to him, 'Every man serves the good wine first, and when the people have drunk freely, then he serves the poorer wine; but you have kept the good wine until now.' This beginning of His signs Jesus did in Cana of Galilee, and manifested His glory, and His disciples believed in Him" (Jn. 2:1-11).

I Do Not Receive Glory from Men

"If I alone testify about Myself, My testimony is not true. There is another who testifies of Me, and I know that the testimony which He gives about Me is true. You have sent to John, and he has testified to the truth. But the testimony which I receive is not from man, but I say these things so that you may be saved. He was the lamp that was burning and was shining and you were willing to rejoice for a while in his light. But the testimony which I have is greater than the testimony of John; for the works which the Father has given Me to accomplish—the very works that I do—testify about Me, that the Father has sent Me. And the Father who sent Me, He has testified of Me. You have neither heard His voice at any time nor seen His form. You do not have His word abiding in you, for you do not believe Him whom He sent. You search the Scriptures because you think that in them you have eternal life; it is these that testify about Me; and you are unwilling to come to Me so that you may have life. I do not receive glory from men; but I know you, that you do not have the love of God in yourselves. I have come in My Father's name, and you do not receive Me; if another comes in his own name, you will receive him. How can you believe, when you receive glory from one another and you do not seek the glory that is from the one and only God? Do not think that I will accuse you before the Father; the one who accuses you is Moses, in whom you have set your hope. For if you believed Moses, you would believe Me, for he wrote about Me. But if you do not believe his writings, how will you believe My words" (Jn. 5:31-47)?

He Who Speaks from Himself Seeks His Own Glory

"But when it was now the midst of the feast Jesus went up into the temple, and began to teach. The Jews then were astonished, saying, 'How has this man become learned, having never been educated?' So Jesus answered them and said, 'My teaching is not Mine, but

His who sent Me. If anyone is willing to do His will, he will know of the teaching, whether it is of God or whether I speak from Myself. He who speaks from himself seeks his own glory; but He who is seeking the glory of the One who sent Him, He is true, and there is no unrighteousness in Him"' (Jn. 7:14-18).

I Do Not Seek My Glory

"The Jews answered and said to Him, 'Do we not say rightly that You are a Samaritan and have a demon?' Jesus answered, 'I do not have a demon; but I honor My Father, and you dishonor Me. But I do not seek My glory; there is One who seeks and judges. Truly, truly, I say to you, if anyone keeps My word he will never see death.' The Jews said to Him, 'Now we know that You have a demon. Abraham died, and the prophets also; and You say, "If anyone keeps My word, he will never taste of death." Surely You are not greater than our father Abraham, who died? The prophets died too; whom do You make Yourself out to be?' Jesus answered, 'If I glorify Myself, My glory is nothing; it is My Father who glorifies Me, of whom you say, "He is our God"; and you have not come to know Him, but I know Him; and if I say that I do not know Him, I will be a liar like you, but I do know Him and keep His word. Your father Abraham rejoiced to see My day, and he saw it and was glad.' So the Jews said to Him, 'You are not yet fifty years old, and have You seen Abraham?' Jesus said to them, 'Truly, truly, I say to you, before Abraham was born, I am.' Therefore they picked up stones to throw at Him, but Jesus hid Himself and went out of the temple" (Jn. 8:48-59).

Chapter Three

Give Glory to God; We Know that This Man Is
a Sinner

"So a second time they called the man who had been blind, and said to him, 'Give glory to God; we know that this man is a sinner.' He then answered, 'Whether He is a sinner, I do not know; one thing I do know, that though I was blind, now I see.' So they said to him, 'What did He do to you? How did He open your eyes?' He answered them, 'I told you already and you did not listen; why do you want to hear it again? You do not want to become His disciples too, do you?' They reviled him and said, 'You are His disciple, but we are disciples of Moses. We know that God has spoken to Moses, but as for this man, we do not know where He is from.' The man answered and said to them, 'Well, here is an amazing thing, that you do not know where He is from, and yet He opened my eyes. We know that God does not hear sinners; but if anyone is God-fearing and does His will, He hears him. Since the beginning of time it has never been heard that anyone opened the eyes of a person born blind. If this man were not from God, He could do nothing.' They answered him, 'You were born entirely in sins, and are you teaching us?' So they put him out" (Jn. 9:24-34).

For the Glory of God, that the Son of God May Be
Glorified by It

"Now a certain man was sick, Lazarus of Bethany, the village of Mary and her sister Martha. It was the Mary who anointed the Lord with ointment, and wiped His feet with her hair, whose brother Lazarus was sick. So the sisters sent word to Him, saying, 'Lord, behold, he whom You love is sick.' But when Jesus heard this, He said, 'This sickness is not to end in death, but for the glory of God, so that the Son of God may be glorified by it.' Now Jesus loved Martha and her sister and Lazarus. So when He heard that he was sick, He then stayed two days longer in the place where He was. Then after this He said to the disciples, 'Let us go to Judea again.' The disciples said to Him, 'Rabbi, the Jews were just now seeking to stone You, and are You going there again?' Jesus answered, 'Are there not twelve hours in the day? If anyone walks in the day, he does not stumble, because he sees the light of this world. But if anyone walks in the night, he stumbles, because the light is not in him.' This He said, and after that He said to them, 'Our friend Lazarus has fallen asleep; but I go, so that I may awaken him out of sleep.' The disciples then said to Him, 'Lord, if he has fallen asleep, he will recover.' Now Jesus had spoken of his death, but they thought that He was speaking of literal sleep. So Jesus then said to them plainly, 'Lazarus is dead, and I am glad for your sakes that I was not there, so that you may believe; but let us go to him.' Therefore Thomas, who is called Didymus, said to his fellow disciples, 'Let us also go, so that we may die with Him'" (Jn. 11:1-16).

If You Believe, You Will See the Glory of God

"So Jesus, again being deeply moved within, came to the tomb. Now it was a cave, and a stone was lying against it. Jesus said, 'Remove the stone.' Martha, the sister of the deceased, said to Him, 'Lord, by this time there will be a stench, for he has been dead four days.' Jesus said to her, 'Did I not say to you that if you believe, you will see the glory of God?' So they removed the stone. Then Jesus raised His eyes, and said, 'Father, I thank You that You have heard Me. I knew that You always hear Me; but because of the people standing around I said it, so that they may believe that You sent Me.' When He had said these things, He cried out with a loud voice, 'Lazarus, come forth.' The man who had died came forth, bound hand and foot with wrappings, and his face was wrapped around with a cloth. Jesus said to them, 'Unbind him, and let him go'" (Jn. 11:38-44).

The Glory Which I Had with Thee Before the World Was

"Jesus spoke these things; and lifting up His eyes to heaven, He said, 'Father, the hour has come; glorify Your Son, that the Son may glorify You, even as You gave Him authority over all flesh, that to all whom You have given Him, He may give eternal life. This is eternal life, that they may know You, the only true God, and Jesus Christ whom You have sent. I glorified You on the earth, having accomplished the work which You have given Me to do. Now, Father, glorify Me together with Yourself, with the glory which I had with You before the world was'" (Jn. 17:1-5).

The Glory Which Thou Hast Given Me

"I do not ask on behalf of these alone, but for those also who believe in Me through their word; that they may all be one; even as You, Father, are in Me and I in You, that they also may be in Us, so that the world may believe that You sent Me. The glory which You have given Me I have given to them, that they may be one, just as We are one; I in them and You in Me, that they may be perfected in unity, so that the world may know that You sent Me, and loved them, even as You have loved Me. Father, I desire that they also, whom You have given Me, be with Me where I am, so that they may see My glory which You have given Me, for You loved Me before the foundation of the world" (Jn. 17:20-24).

IN THE BOOK OF ACTS

The God of Glory Appeared to Our Father Abraham

"And he said, 'Hear me, brethren and fathers! The God of glory appeared to our father Abraham when he was in Mesopotamia, before he lived in Haran, and said to him, "LEAVE YOUR COUNTRY AND YOUR RELATIVES, AND COME INTO THE LAND THAT I WILL SHOW YOU." Then he left the land of the Chaldeans and settled in Haran. From there, after his father died, God had him move to this country in which you are now living. But He gave him no inheritance in it, not even a foot of ground, and yet, even when he had no child, He promised that HE WOULD GIVE IT TO HIM AS A POSSESSION, AND TO HIS DESCENDANTS AFTER HIM. But God spoke to this effect, that his DESCENDANTS WOULD BE ALIENS IN A FOREIGN LAND, AND THAT THEY WOULD BE ENSLAVED AND MISTREATED FOR FOUR HUNDRED YEARS. "AND WHATEVER NATION TO WHICH THEY WILL BE IN BONDAGE I MYSELF WILL JUDGE," said God, "AND AFTER THAT THEY WILL COME OUT AND SERVE ME IN THIS PLACE."

Chapter Three

And He gave him the covenant of circumcision; and so Abraham became the father of Isaac, and circumcised him on the eighth day; and Isaac became the father of Jacob, and Jacob of the twelve patriarchs"" (Ac. 7:2-8).

He Gazed Intently into Heaven and Saw the Glory of God

"Now when they heard this, they were cut to the quick, and they began gnashing their teeth at him. But being full of the Holy Spirit, he gazed intently into heaven and saw the glory of God, and Jesus standing at the right hand of God; and he said, 'Behold, I see the heavens opened up and the Son of Man standing at the right hand of God.' But they cried out with a loud voice, and covered their ears and rushed at him with one impulse. When they had driven him out of the city, they began stoning him;and the witnesses laid aside their robes at the feet of a young man named Saul. They went on stoning Stephen as he called on the Lord and said, 'Lord Jesus, receive my spirit!' Then falling on his knees, he cried out with a loud voice, 'Lord, do not hold this sin against them!' Having said this, he fell asleep" (Ac. 7:54-60).

An Angel of the Lord Struck Him Because He Did Not Give God the Glory

"Now he was very angry with the people of Tyre and Sidon; and with one accord they came to him, and having won over Blastus the king's chamberlain, they were asking for peace, because their country was fed by the king's country. On an appointed day Herod, having put on his royal apparel, took his seat on the rostrum and began delivering an address to them. The people kept crying out, 'The voice of a god and not of a man!' And immediately an angel of the Lord struck him because he did not give God the glory, and he was eaten by worms and died" (Ac. 12:20-23).

IN THE BOOK OF ROMANS

The Became Fouls and Exchanged the Glory of the Incorruptible God

"For the wrath of God is revealed from heaven against all ungodliness and unrighteousness of men who suppress the truth in unrighteousness, because that which is known about God is evident within them; for God made it evident to them. For since the creation of the world His invisible attributes, His eternal power and divine nature, have been clearly seen, being understood through what has been made, so that they are without excuse. For even though they knew God, they did not honor Him as God or give thanks, but they became futile in their speculations, and their foolish heart was darkened. Professing to be wise, they became fools, and exchanged the glory of the incorruptible God for an image in the form of corruptible man and of birds and four-footed animals and crawling creatures" (Ro. 1:18-23).

The Truth of God Abounded to His Glory

"Then what advantage has the Jew? Or what is the benefit of circumcision? Great in every respect. First of all, that they were entrusted with the oracles of God. What then? If some did not believe, their unbelief will not nullify the faithfulness of God, will it? May it never be! Rather, let God be found true, though every man be found a liar, as it is written, 'THAT YOU MAY BE JUSTIFIED IN YOUR WORDS, AND PREVAIL WHEN YOU ARE JUDGED.' But if our unrighteousness demonstrates the righteousness of God, what shall we say? The God who inflicts wrath is not unrighteous, is He? (I am speaking in human terms.) May it never be! For otherwise, how will God judge the world? But if through my lie the truth of God abounded to His glory, why am I also still being judged as a sinner? And why not say (as we are slanderously reported and as some claim that we say), 'Let us do evil that good may come'? Their condemnation is just" (Ro. 3:1-8).

All Have Sinned and Fall Short of the Glory of God

"But now apart from the Law the righteousness of God has been manifested, being witnessed by the Law and the Prophets, even the righteousness of God through faith in Jesus Christ for all those who believe; for there is no distinction; for all have sinned and fall short of the glory of God, being justified as a gift by His grace through the redemption which is in Christ Jesus; whom God displayed publicly as a propitiation in His blood through faith. This was to demonstrate His righteousness, because in the forbearance of God He passed over the sins previously committed; for the demonstration, I say, of His righteousness at the present time, so that He would be just and the justifier of the one who has faith in Jesus" (Ro. 3:21-26).

Chapter Three

He Did Not Waver in Unbelief, but Grew Strong in Faith, Giving Glory to God

"For this reason it is by faith, in order that it may be in accordance with grace, so that the promise will be guaranteed to all the descendants, not only to those who are of the Law, but also to those who are of the faith of Abraham, who is the father of us all, (as it is written, 'A FATHER OF MANY NATIONS HAVE I MADE YOU') in the presence of Him whom he believed, even God, who gives life to the dead and calls into being that which does not exist. In hope against hope he believed, so that he might become a father of many nations according to that which had been spoken, 'SO SHALL YOUR DESCENDANTS BE.' Without becoming weak in faith he contemplated his own body, now as good as dead since he was about a hundred years old, and the deadness of Sarah's womb; yet, with respect to the promise of God, he did not waver in unbelief but grew strong in faith, giving glory to God, and being fully assured that what God had promised, He was able also to perform. Therefore IT WAS ALSO CREDITED TO HIM AS RIGHTEOUSNESS. Now not for his sake only was it written that it was credited to him, but for our sake also, to whom it will be credited, as those who believe in Him who raised Jesus our Lord from the dead, He who was delivered over because of our transgressions, and was raised because of our justification" (Ro. 4:16-25).

We Exult in Hope of the Glory of God

"Therefore, having been justified by faith, we have peace with God through our Lord Jesus Christ, through whom also we have obtained our introduction by faith into this grace in which we stand; and we exult in hope of the glory of God. And not only this, but we also exult in our tribulations, knowing that tribulation brings about perseverance; and perseverance, proven character; and proven character, hope; and hope does not disappoint, because the love of God has been poured out within our hearts through the Holy Spirit who was given to us" (Ro. 5:1-5).

Christ Was Raised from the Dead through the Glory of the Father

"What shall we say then? Are we to continue in sin so that grace may increase? May it never be! How shall we who died to sin still live in it? Or do you not know that all of us who have been baptized into Christ Jesus have been baptized into His death? Therefore we have been buried with Him through baptism into death, so that as Christ was raised from the dead through the glory of the Father, so we too might walk in newness of life. For if we have become united with Him in the likeness of His death, certainly we shall also be in the likeness of His resurrection, knowing this, that our old self was crucified with Him, in order that our body of sin might be done away with, so that we would no longer be slaves to sin; for he who has died is freed from sin" (Ro. 6:1-7).

The Glory That Is to Be Revealed to Us

"For I consider that the sufferings of this present time are not worthy to be compared with the glory that is to be revealed to us. For the anxious longing of the creation waits eagerly for the revealing of the sons of God. For the creation was subjected to futility, not willingly, but because of Him who subjected it, in hope that the creation itself also will be set free from its slavery to corruption into the freedom of the glory of the children of God. For we know that the whole creation groans and suffers the pains of childbirth together until now. And not only this, but also we ourselves, having the first fruits of the Spirit, even we ourselves groan within ourselves, waiting eagerly for our adoption as sons, the redemption of our body. For in hope we have been saved, but hope that is seen is not hope; for who hopes for what he already sees? But if we hope for what we do not see, with perseverance we wait eagerly for it. In the same way the Spirit also helps our weakness; for we do not know how to pray as we should, but the Spirit Himself intercedes for us with groanings too deep for words; and He who searches the hearts knows what the mind of the Spirit is, because He intercedes for the saints according to the will of God" (Ro. 8:18-27).

He Might Make Known the Riches of His Glory Upon Vessels of Mercy

"You will say to me then, 'Why does He still find fault? For who resists His will?' On the contrary, who are you, O man, who answers back to God? The thing molded will not say to the molder, 'Why did you make me like this,' will it? Or does not the potter have a right over the clay, to make from the same lump one vessel for honorable use and another for common use? What if God, although willing to demonstrate His wrath and to make His power known, endured with much patience vessels of wrath prepared for destruction? And He did so to make known the riches of His glory upon vessels of mercy, which He prepared beforehand for glory, even us, whom He also called, not from among Jews only, but also from among Gentiles. As He says also in Hosea, 'I WILL CALL THOSE WHO WERE NOT MY PEOPLE, "MY PEOPLE," AND HER WHO WAS NOT BELOVED, "BELOVED."' 'AND IT SHALL BE THAT IN THE PLACE WHERE IT WAS SAID TO THEM, "YOU ARE NOT MY PEOPLE," THERE THEY SHALL BE CALLED SONS OF THE LIVING GOD'" (Ro. 9:19-26).

To Him Be the Glory Forever

"Oh, the depth of the riches both of the wisdom and knowledge of God! How unsearchable are His judgments and unfathomable His ways! For WHO HAS KNOWN THE MIND OF THE LORD, OR WHO BECAME HIS COUNSELOR? Or WHO HAS FIRST GIVEN TO HIM THAT IT MIGHT BE PAID BACK TO HIM AGAIN? For from Him and through Him and to Him are all things. To Him be the glory forever. Amen" (Ro. 11:33-36).

Accept One Another, Just as Christ Also Accepted Us to the Glory of God

"Therefore, accept one another, just as Christ also accepted us to the glory of God. For I say that Christ has become a servant to the circumcision on behalf of the truth of God to confirm the promises given to the fathers, and for the Gentiles to glorify God for His mercy; as it is written, 'THEREFORE I WILL GIVE

PRAISE TO YOU AMONG THE GENTILES, AND I WILL SING TO YOUR NAME.' Again he says, 'REJOICE, O GENTILES, WITH HIS PEOPLE.' And again, 'PRAISE THE LORD ALL YOU GENTILES, AND LET ALL THE PEOPLES PRAISE HIM.' Again Isaiah says, 'THERE SHALL COME THE ROOT OF JESSE, AND HE WHO ARISES TO RULE OVER THE GENTILES, IN HIM SHALL THE GENTILES HOPE.' Now may the God of hope fill you with all joy and peace in believing, so that you will abound in hope by the power of the Holy Spirit. And concerning you, my brethren, I myself also am convinced that you yourselves are full of goodness, filled with all knowledge and able also to admonish one another" (Ro. 15:7-14).

To the Only Wise God, Through Jesus Christ, Be the Glory Forever

"Now to Him who is able to establish you according to my gospel and the preaching of Jesus Christ, according to the revelation of the mystery which has been kept secret for long ages past, but now is manifested, and by the Scriptures of the prophets, according to the commandment of the eternal God, has been made known to all the nations, leading to obedience of faith; to the only wise God, through Jesus Christ, be the glory forever. Amen" (Ro. 16:25-27).

Chapter Three

IN THE BOOK OF 1 CORINTHIANS

Which God Predestined Before the Ages to Our Glory

"Yet we do speak wisdom among those who are mature; a wisdom, however, not of this age nor of the rulers of this age, who are passing away; but we speak God's wisdom in a mystery, the hidden wisdom which God predestined before the ages to our glory; the wisdom which none of the rulers of this age has understood; for if they had understood it they would not have crucified the Lord of glory; but just as it is written, 'THINGS WHICH EYE HAS NOT SEEN AND EAR HAS NOT HEARD, AND which HAVE NOT ENTERED THE HEART OF MAN, ALL THAT GOD HAS PREPARED FOR THOSE WHO LOVE HIM.' For to us God revealed them through the Spirit; for the Spirit searches all things, even the depths of God. For who among men knows the thoughts of a man except the spirit of the man which is in him? Even so the thoughts of God no one knows except the Spirit of God. Now we have received, not the spirit of the world, but the Spirit who is from God, so that we may know the things freely given to us by God, which things we also speak, not in words taught by human wisdom, but in those taught by the Spirit, combining spiritual thoughts with spiritual words" (1Co. 2:6-13).

Whatever You Do, Do All to the Glory of God

"Whether, then, you eat or drink or whatever you do, do all to the glory of God. Give no offense either to Jews or to Greeks or to the church of God; just as I also please all men in all things, not seeking my own profit but the profit of the many, so that they may be saved" (1Co. 10:31-33).

He Is the Image and Glory of God

"Now I praise you because you remember me in everything and hold firmly to the traditions, just as I delivered them to you. But I want you to understand that Christ is the head of every man, and the man is the head of a woman, and God is the head of Christ. Every man who has something on his head while praying or prophesying disgraces his head. But every woman who has her head uncovered while praying or prophesying disgraces her head, for she is one and the same as the woman whose head is shaved. For if a woman does not cover her head, let her also have her hair cut off; but if it is disgraceful for a woman to have her hair cut off or her head shaved, let her cover her head. For a man ought not to have his head covered, since he is the image and glory of God; but the woman is the glory of man. For man does not originate from woman, but woman from man; for indeed man was not created for the woman's sake, but woman for the man's sake. Therefore the woman ought to have a symbol of authority on her head, because of the angels. However, in the Lord, neither is woman independent of man, nor is man independent of woman. For as the woman originates from the man, so also the man has his birth through the woman; and all things originate from God. Judge for yourselves: is it proper for a woman to pray to God with her head uncovered? Does not even nature itself teach you that if a man has long hair, it is a dishonor to him, but if a woman has long hair, it is a glory to her? For her hair is given to her for a covering. But if one is inclined to be contentious, we have no other practice, nor have the churches of God" (1Co. 11:2-16).

IN THE BOOK OF 2 CORINTHIANS

The Glory of God Through Us

"In this confidence I intended at first to come to you, so that you might twice receive a blessing; that is, to pass your way into Macedonia, and again from Macedonia to come to you, and by you to be helped on my journey to Judea. Therefore, I was not vacillating when I intended to do this, was I? Or what I purpose, do I purpose according to the flesh, so that with me there will be yes, yes and no, no at the same time? But as God is faithful, our word to you is not yes and no. For the Son of God, Christ Jesus, who was preached among you by us — by me and Silvanus and Timothy — was not yes and no, but is yes in Him. For as many as are the promises of God, in Him they are yes; therefore also through Him is our Amen to the glory of God through us. Now He who establishes us with you in Christ and anointed us is God, who also sealed us and gave us the Spirit in our hearts as a pledge" (2Co. 1:15-22).

From Glory to Glory

"Therefore having such a hope, we use great boldness in our speech, and are not like Moses, who used to put a veil over his face so that the sons of Israel would not look intently at the end of what was fading away. But their minds were hardened; for until this very day at the reading of the old covenant the same veil remains unlifted, because it is removed in Christ. But to this day whenever Moses is read, a veil lies over their heart; but whenever a person turns to the Lord, the veil is taken away. Now the Lord is the Spirit, and where the Spirit of the Lord is, there is liberty. But we all, with unveiled face, beholding as in a mirror the glory of the Lord, are being transformed into the same image from glory to glory, just as from the Lord, the Spirit" (2Co. 3:12-18).

That They Might Not See the Light of the Gospel of the Glory of Christ

"Therefore, since we have this ministry, as we received mercy, we do not lose heart, but we have renounced the things hidden because of shame, not walking in craftiness or adulterating the word of God, but by the manifestation of truth commending ourselves to every man's conscience in the sight of God. And even if our gospel is veiled, it is veiled to those who are perishing, in whose case the god of this world has blinded the minds of the unbelieving so that they might not see the light of the gospel of the glory of Christ, who is the image of God. For we do not preach ourselves but Christ Jesus as Lord, and ourselves as your bond-servants for Jesus' sake. For God, who said, 'Light shall shine out of darkness,' is the One who has shone in our hearts to give the Light of the knowledge of the glory of God in the face of Christ" (2Co. 4:1-6).

The Giving of Thanks to Abound to the Glory of God

"But having the same spirit of faith, according to what is written, 'I BELIEVED, THEREFORE I SPOKE,' we also believe, therefore we also speak, knowing that

Chapter Three

He who raised the Lord Jesus will raise us also with Jesus and will present us with you. For all things are for your sakes, so that the grace which is spreading to more and more people may cause the giving of thanks to abound to the glory of God" (2Co. 4:13-15).

For the Glory of the Lord Himself

"But thanks be to God who puts the same earnestness on your behalf in the heart of Titus. For he not only accepted our appeal, but being himself very earnest, he has gone to you of his own accord. We have sent along with him the brother whose fame in the things of the gospel has spread through all the churches; and not only this, but he has also been appointed by the churches to travel with us in this gracious work, which is being administered by us for the glory of the Lord Himself, and to show our readiness, taking precaution so that no one will discredit us in our administration of this generous gift; for we have regard for what is honorable, not only in the sight of the Lord, but also in the sight of men. We have sent with them our brother, whom we have often tested and found diligent in many things, but now even more diligent because of his great confidence in you. As for Titus, he is my partner and fellow worker among you; as for our brethren, they are messengers of the churches, a glory to Christ. Therefore openly before the churches, show them the proof of your love and of our reason for boasting about you" (2Co. 8:16-24).

Chapter Three

IN THE BOOK OF GALATIANS

To Whom Be the Glory Forevermore

"Grace to you and peace from God our Father and the Lord Jesus Christ, who gave Himself for our sins so that He might rescue us from this present evil age, according to the will of our God and Father, to whom be the glory forevermore. Amen" (Gal. 1:3-5).

IN THE BOOK OF EPHESIANS

To the Praise of the Glory of His Grace

"Blessed be the God and Father of our Lord Jesus Christ, who has blessed us with every spiritual blessing in the heavenly places in Christ, just as He chose us in Him before the foundation of the world, that we would be holy and blameless before Him. In love He predestined us to adoption as sons through Jesus Christ to Himself, according to the kind intention of His will, to the praise of the glory of His grace, which He freely bestowed on us in the Beloved. In Him we have redemption through His blood, the forgiveness of our trespasses, according to the riches of His grace which He lavished on us. In all wisdom and insight He made known to us the mystery of His will, according to His kind intention which He purposed in Him with a view to an administration suitable to the fullness of the times, that is, the summing up of all things in Christ, things in the heavens and things on the earth. In Him also we have obtained an inheritance, having been predestined according to His purpose who works all things after the counsel of His will, to the end that we who were the first to hope in Christ would be to the praise of His glory. In Him, you also, after listening to the message of truth, the gospel of your salvation—having also believed, you were sealed in Him with the Holy Spirit of promise, who is given as a pledge of our inheritance, with a view to the redemption of God's own possession, to the praise of His glory" (Eph. 1:3-14).

The Riches of the Glory of His Inheritance in the Saints

"For this reason I too, having heard of the faith in the Lord Jesus which exists among you and your love for all the saints, do not cease giving thanks for you, while making mention of you in my prayers; that the God of our Lord Jesus Christ, the Father of glory, may give to you a spirit of wisdom and of revelation in the knowledge of Him. I pray that the eyes of your heart may be enlightened, so that you will know what is the hope of His calling, what are the riches of the glory of His inheritance in the saints, and what is the surpassing greatness of His power toward us who believe. These are in accordance with the working of the strength of His might which He brought about in Christ, when He raised Him from the dead and seated Him at His right hand in the heavenly places, far above all rule and authority and power and dominion, and every name that is named, not only in this age but also in the one to come. And He put all things in subjection under His feet, and gave Him as head over all things to the church, which is His body, the fullness of Him who fills all in all" (Eph. 1:15-23).

Chapter Three

According to the Riches of His Glory, to Be Strengthened with Power

"For this reason I bow my knees before the Father, from whom every family in heaven and on earth derives its name, that He would grant you, according to the riches of His glory, to be strengthened with power through His Spirit in the inner man, so that Christ may dwell in your hearts through faith; and that you, being rooted and grounded in love, may be able to comprehend with all the saints what is the breadth and length and height and depth, and to know the love of Christ which surpasses knowledge, that you may be filled up to all the fullness of God" (Eph. 3:14-19).

To Him Be the Glory in the Church

"Now to Him who is able to do far more abundantly beyond all that we ask or think, according to the power that works within us, to Him be the glory in the church and in Christ Jesus to all generations forever and ever. Amen" (Eph. 3:20-21).

IN THE BOOK OF PHILIPPIANS

The Fruit of Righteousness Which Comes Through Jesus Christ, to the Glory and Praise of God

"I thank my God in all my remembrance of you, always offering prayer with joy in my every prayer for you all, in view of your participation in the gospel from the first day until now. For I am confident of this very thing, that He who began a good work in you will perfect it until the day of Christ Jesus. For it is only right for me to feel this way about you all, because I have you in my heart, since both in my imprisonment and in the defense and confirmation of the gospel, you all are partakers of grace with me. For God is my witness, how I long for you all with the affection of Christ Jesus. And this I pray, that your love may abound still more and more in real knowledge and all discernment, so that you may approve the things that are excellent, in order to be sincere and blameless until the day of Christ; having been filled with the fruit of righteousness which comes through Jesus Christ, to the glory and praise of God" (Php. 1:3-11).

Every Tongue Should Confess that Jesus Christ Is Lord, to the Glory of God the Father

"Therefore if there is any encouragement in Christ, if there is any consolation of love, if there is any fellowship of the Spirit, if any affection and compassion, make my joy complete by being of the same mind, maintaining the same love, united in spirit, intent on one purpose. Do nothing from selfishness or empty conceit, but with humility of mind regard one another as more important than yourselves; do not merely look out for your own personal interests, but also for the interests of others. Have this attitude in yourselves which was also in Christ Jesus, who, although He existed in the form of God, did not regard equality with God a thing to be grasped, but emptied Himself, taking the form of a bond-servant, and being made in the likeness of men. Being found in appearance as a man, He humbled Himself by becoming obedient to the point of death, even death on a cross. For this reason also, God highly exalted Him, and bestowed on Him the name which is above every name, so that at the name of Jesus EVERY KNEE WILL BOW, of those who are in heaven and on earth and under the earth, and that every tongue will confess that Jesus Christ is Lord, to the glory of God the Father" (Php. 2:1-11).

Who Worship in the Spirit of God and Glory in Christ Jesus

"Beware of the dogs, beware of the evil workers, beware of the false circumcision; for we are the true circumcision, who worship in the Spirit of God and glory in Christ Jesus and put no confidence in the flesh, although I myself might have confidence even in the flesh. If anyone else has a mind to put confidence in the flesh, I far more: circumcised the eighth day, of the nation of Israel, of the tribe of Benjamin, a Hebrew of Hebrews; as to the Law, a Pharisee; as to zeal, a persecutor of the church; as to the righteousness which is in the Law, found blameless" (Php. 3:2-6).

Into Conformity with the Body of His Glory

"Brethren, join in following my example, and observe those who walk according to the pattern you have in us. For many walk, of whom I often told you, and now tell you even weeping, that they are enemies of the cross of Christ, whose end is destruction, whose god is their appetite, and whose glory is in their shame, who set their minds on earthly things. For our citizenship is in heaven, from which also we eagerly wait for a Savior, the Lord Jesus Christ; who will transform the body of our humble state into conformity with the body of His glory, by the exertion of the power that He has even to subject all things to Himself" (Php. 3:17-21).

God Shall Supply All Your Needs According to His Riches in Glory in Christ Jesus

"You yourselves also know, Philippians, that at the first preaching of the gospel, after I left Macedonia, no church shared with me in the matter of giving and receiving but you alone; for even in Thessalonica you sent a gift more than once for my needs. Not that I seek the gift itself, but I seek for the profit which increases to your account. But I have received everything in full and have an abundance; I am amply supplied, having received from Epaphroditus what you have sent, a fragrant aroma, an acceptable sacrifice, well-pleasing to God. And my God will supply all your needs according to His riches in glory in Christ Jesus. Now to our God and Father be the glory forever and ever. Amen" (Php. 4:15-20).

IN THE BOOK OF COLOSSIANS

This Mystery Among the Gentiles, Which Is Christ in You, the Hope of Glory

"Now I rejoice in my sufferings for your sake, and in my flesh I do my share on behalf of His body, which is the church, in filling up what is lacking in Christ's afflictions. Of this church I was made a minister according to the stewardship from God bestowed on me for your benefit, so that I might fully carry out the preaching of the word of God, that is, the mystery which has been hidden from the past ages and generations, but has now been manifested to His saints, to whom God willed to make known what is the riches of the glory of this mystery among the Gentiles, which is Christ in you, the hope of glory. We proclaim Him, admonishing every man and teaching every man with all wisdom, so that we may present every man complete in Christ. For this purpose also I labor, striving according to His power, which mightily works within me" (Col. 1:24-29).

When Christ, Who Is Our Life, Is Revealed, Then You Also Will Be Revealed with Him in Glory

"Therefore if you have been raised up with Christ, keep seeking the things above, where Christ is, seated at the right hand of God. Set your mind on the things above, not on the things that are on earth. For you have died and your life is hidden with Christ in God. When Christ, who is our life, is revealed, then you also will be revealed with Him in glory" (Col. 3:1-4).

IN THE BOOK OF 1 THESSALONIANS

Walk in a Manner Worthy of the God Who Calls You into His Own Kingdom and Glory

"For you recall, brethren, our labor and hardship, how working night and day so as not to be a burden to any of you, we proclaimed to you the gospel of God. You are witnesses, and so is God, how devoutly and uprightly and blamelessly we behaved toward you believers; just as you know how we were exhorting and encouraging and imploring each one of you as a father would his own children, so that you would walk in a manner worthy of the God who calls you into His own kingdom and glory" (1Th. 2:9-12).

IN THE BOOK OF THESSALONIANS

Away from the Presence of the Lord and from the Glory of His Power

"We ought always to give thanks to God for you, brethren, as is only fitting, because your faith is greatly enlarged, and the love of each one of you toward one another grows ever greater; therefore, we ourselves speak proudly of you among the churches of God for your perseverance and faith in the midst of all your persecutions and afflictions which you endure. This is a plain indication of God's righteous judgment so that you will be considered worthy of the kingdom of God, for which indeed you are suffering. For after all it is only just for God to repay with affliction those who afflict you, and to give relief to you who are afflicted and to us as well when the Lord Jesus will be revealed from heaven with His mighty angels in flaming fire, dealing out retribution to those who do not know God and to those who do not obey the gospel of our Lord Jesus. These will pay the penalty of eternal destruction, away from the presence of the Lord and from the glory of His power, when He comes to be glorified in His saints on that day, and to be marveled at among all who have believed—for our testimony to you was believed. To this end also we pray for you always, that our God will count you worthy of your calling, and fulfill every desire for goodness and the work of faith with power, so that the name of our Lord Jesus will be glorified in you, and you in Him, according to the grace of our God and the Lord Jesus Christ" (2Th. 1:3-12).

Chapter Three

That You May Gain the Glory of Our Lord Jesus Christ

"But we should always give thanks to God for you, brethren beloved by the Lord, because God has chosen you from the beginning for salvation through sanctification by the Spirit and faith in the truth. It was for this He called you through our gospel, that you may gain the glory of our Lord Jesus Christ. So then, brethren, stand firm and hold to the traditions which you were taught, whether by word of mouth or by letter from us" (2Th. 2:13-15).

IN THE BOOK OF 1 TIMOTHY

The Only God, Be Honor and Glory Forever and Ever

"I thank Christ Jesus our Lord, who has strengthened me, because He considered me faithful, putting me into service, even though I was formerly a blasphemer and a persecutor and a violent aggressor. Yet I was shown mercy because I acted ignorantly in unbelief; and the grace of our Lord was more than abundant, with the faith and love which are found in Christ Jesus. It is a trustworthy statement, deserving full acceptance, that Christ Jesus came into the world to save sinners, among whom I am foremost of all. Yet for this reason I found mercy, so that in me as the foremost, Jesus Christ might demonstrate His perfect patience as an example for those who would believe in Him for eternal life. Now to the King eternal, immortal, invisible, the only God, be honor and glory forever and ever. Amen" (1Ti. 1:12-17).

Chapter Three

IN THE BOOK OF 2 TIMOTHY

He Will Bring Me Safely to His Heavenly Kingdom; to Him Be the Glory

"At my first defense no one supported me, but all deserted me; may it not be counted against them. But the Lord stood with me and strengthened me, so that through me the proclamation might be fully accomplished, and that all the Gentiles might hear; and I was rescued out of the lion's mouth. The Lord will rescue me from every evil deed, and will bring me safely to His heavenly kingdom; to Him be the glory forever and ever. Amen" (2Ti. 4:16-18).

IN THE BOOK OF TITUS

Looking for the Blessed Hope and the Appearing of the Glory of Our Great God and Savior

"For the grace of God has appeared, bringing salvation to all men, instructing us to deny ungodliness and worldly desires and to live sensibly, righteously and godly in the present age, looking for the blessed hope and the appearing of the glory of our great God and Savior, Christ Jesus, who gave Himself for us to redeem us from every lawless deed, and to purify for Himself a people for His own possession, zealous for good deeds" (Tit. 2:11-14).

Chapter Three

IN THE BOOK OF HEBREWS

He Is the Radiance of His Glory and the Exact Representation of His Nature

"God, after He spoke long ago to the fathers in the prophets in many portions and in many ways, in these last days has spoken to us in His Son, whom He appointed heir of all things, through whom also He made the world. And He is the radiance of His glory and the exact representation of His nature, and upholds all things by the word of His power. When He had made purification of sins, He sat down at the right hand of the Majesty on high, having become as much better than the angels, as He has inherited a more excellent name than they" (Heb. 1:1-4).

Crowned Him with Glory and Honor, and Hast Appointed Him Over the Works of Thy Hands

"For He did not subject to angels the world to come, concerning which we are speaking. But one has testified somewhere, saying, 'WHAT IS MAN, THAT YOU REMEMBER HIM? OR THE SON OF MAN, THAT YOU ARE CONCERNED ABOUT HIM? YOU HAVE MADE HIM FOR A LITTLE WHILE LOWER THAN THE ANGELS; YOU HAVE CROWNED HIM WITH GLORY AND HONOR, AND HAVE APPOINTED HIM OVER THE WORKS OF YOUR HANDS; YOU HAVE PUT ALL THINGS IN SUBJECTION UNDER HIS FEET.' For in subjecting all things to him, He left nothing that is not subject to him. But now we do not yet see all things subjected to him. But we do see Him who was made for a little while lower than the angels, namely, Jesus, because of the suffering of death crowned with glory and honor, so that by the grace of God He might taste death for everyone" (Heb. 2:5-9).

He Has Been Counted Worthy of More Glory Than Moses

"Therefore, holy brethren, partakers of a heavenly calling, consider Jesus, the Apostle and High Priest of our confession; He was faithful to Him who appointed Him, as Moses also was in all His house. For He has been counted worthy of more glory than Moses, by just so much as the builder of the house has more honor than the house. For every house is built by someone, but the builder of all things is God. Now Moses was faithful in all His house as a servant, for a testimony of those things which were to be spoken later; but Christ was faithful as a Son over His house – whose house we are, if we hold fast our confidence and the boast of our hope firm until the end" (Heb. 3:1-6).

Above It Were the Cherubim of Glory Overshadowing the Mercy Seat

"Now even the first covenant had regulations of divine worship and the earthly sanctuary. For there was a tabernacle prepared, the outer one, in which were the lampstand and the table and the sacred bread; this is called the holy place. Behind the second veil there was a tabernacle which is called the Holy of Holies, having a golden altar of incense and the ark of the covenant covered on all sides with gold, in which was a golden jar holding the manna, and Aaron's rod which budded, and the tables of the covenant; and above it were the cherubim of glory overshadowing the mercy seat; but of these things we cannot now speak in detail" (Heb. 9:1-5).

Working in Us that Which Is Pleasing in His Sight, through Jesus Christ, to Whom Be the Glory

"Now the God of peace, who brought up from the dead the great Shepherd of the sheep through the blood of the eternal covenant, even Jesus our Lord, equip you in every good thing to do His will, working in us that which is pleasing in His sight, through Jesus Christ, to whom be the glory forever and ever. Amen" (Heb. 13:20-21).

IN THE BOOK OF 1 PETER

You Greatly Rejoice with Joy Inexpressible and Full of Glory

"Blessed be the God and Father of our Lord Jesus Christ, who according to His great mercy has caused us to be born again to a living hope through the resurrection of Jesus Christ from the dead, to obtain an inheritance which is imperishable and undefiled and will not fade away, reserved in heaven for you, who are protected by the power of God through faith for a salvation ready to be revealed in the last time. In this you greatly rejoice, even though now for a little while, if necessary, you have been distressed by various trials, so that the proof of your faith, being more precious than gold which is perishable, even though tested by fire, may be found to result in praise and glory and honor at the revelation of Jesus Christ; and though you have not seen Him, you love Him, and though you do not see Him now, but believe in Him, you greatly rejoice with joy inexpressible and full of glory, obtaining as the outcome of your faith the salvation of your souls" (1Pe. 1:3-9).

Who Raised Him from the Dead and Gave Him Glory

"If you address as Father the One who impartially judges according to each one's work, conduct yourselves in fear during the time of your stay on earth; knowing that you were not redeemed with perishable things like silver or gold from your futile way of life inherited from your forefathers, but with precious blood, as of a lamb unblemished and spotless, the blood of Christ. For He was foreknown before the foundation of the world, but has appeared in these last times for the sake of you who through Him are believers in God, who raised Him from the dead and gave Him glory, so that your faith and hope are in God" (1Pe. 1:17-21).

God May Be Glorified through Jesus Christ, to Whom Belongs the Glory and Dominion

"The end of all things is near; therefore, be of sound judgment and sober spirit for the purpose of prayer. Above all, keep fervent in your love for one another, because love covers a multitude of sins. Be hospitable to one another without complaint. As each one has received a special gift, employ it in serving one another as good stewards of the manifold grace of God. Whoever speaks, is to do so as one who is speaking the utterances of God; whoever serves is to do so as one who is serving by the strength which God supplies; so that in all things God may be glorified through Jesus Christ, to whom belongs the glory and dominion forever and ever. Amen" (1Pe. 4:7-11).

At the Revelation of His Glory, You May Rejoice with Exultation

"Beloved, do not be surprised at the fiery ordeal among you, which comes upon you for your testing, as though some strange thing were happening to you; but to the degree that you share the sufferings of Christ, keep on rejoicing, so that also at the revelation of His glory you may rejoice with exultation. If you are reviled for the name of Christ, you are blessed, because the Spirit of glory and of God rests on you. Make sure that none of you suffers as a murderer, or thief, or evildoer, or a troublesome meddler; but if anyone suffers as a Christian, he is not to be ashamed, but is to glorify God in this name. For it is time for judgment to begin with the household of God; and if it begins with us first, what will be the outcome for those who do not obey the gospel of God? AND IF IT IS WITH DIFFICULTY THAT THE RIGHTEOUS IS SAVED, WHAT WILL BECOME OF THE GODLESS MAN AND THE SINNER? Therefore, those also who suffer according to the will of God shall entrust their souls to a faithful Creator in doing what is right" (1Pe. 4:12-19).

A Partaker Also of the Glory that Is to Be Revealed

"Therefore, I exhort the elders among you, as your fellow elder and witness of the sufferings of Christ, and a partaker also of the glory that is to be revealed, shepherd the flock of God among you, exercising oversight not under compulsion, but voluntarily, according to the will of God; and not for sordid gain, but with eagerness; nor yet as lording it over those allotted to your charge, but proving to be examples to the flock. And when the Chief Shepherd appears, you will receive the unfading crown of glory. You younger men, likewise, be subject to your elders; and all of you, clothe yourselves with humility toward one another, for GOD IS OPPOSED TO THE PROUD, BUT GIVES GRACE TO THE HUMBLE" (1Pe. 5:1-5).

Who Called You to His Eternal Glory in Christ, Will Himself Perfect, Confirm, Strengthen and Establish You

"Therefore humble yourselves under the mighty hand of God, that He may exalt you at the proper time, casting all your anxiety on Him, because He cares for you. Be of sober spirit, be on the alert. Your adversary, the devil, prowls around like a roaring lion, seeking someone to devour. But resist him, firm in your faith, knowing that the same experiences of suffering are being accomplished by your brethren who are in the world. After you have suffered for a little while, the God of all grace, who called you to His eternal glory in Christ, will Himself perfect, confirm, strengthen and establish you. To Him be dominion forever and ever. Amen" (1Pe. 5:6-11).

Chapter Three

IN THE BOOK OF 2 PETER

Who Called Us by His Own Glory and Excellence

"Simon Peter, a bond-servant and apostle of Jesus Christ, To those who have received a faith of the same kind as ours, by the righteousness of our God and Savior, Jesus Christ: Grace and peace be multiplied to you in the knowledge of God and of Jesus our Lord; seeing that His divine power has granted to us everything pertaining to life and godliness, through the true knowledge of Him who called us by His own glory and excellence. For by these He has granted to us His precious and magnificent promises, so that by them you may become partakers of the divine nature, having escaped the corruption that is in the world by lust. Now for this very reason also, applying all diligence, in your faith supply moral excellence, and in your moral excellence, knowledge, and in your knowledge, self-control, and in your self-control, perseverance, and in your perseverance, godliness, and in your godliness, brotherly kindness, and in your brotherly kindness, love. For if these qualities are yours and are increasing, they render you neither useless nor unfruitful in the true knowledge of our Lord Jesus Christ. For he who lacks these qualities is blind or short-sighted, having forgotten his purification from his former sins. Therefore, brethren, be all the more diligent to make certain about His calling and choosing you; for as long as you practice these things, you will never stumble; for in this way the entrance into the eternal kingdom of our Lord and Savior Jesus Christ will be abundantly supplied to you" (2Pe. 1:1-11).

Chapter Three

He Received Honor and Glory from God the Father

"For we did not follow cleverly devised tales when we made known to you the power and coming of our Lord Jesus Christ, but we were eyewitnesses of His majesty. For when He received honor and glory from God the Father, such an utterance as this was made to Him by the Majestic Glory, 'This is My beloved Son with whom I am well-pleased' — and we ourselves heard this utterance made from heaven when we were with Him on the holy mountain" (2Pe. 1:16-18).

To Him Be the Glory, Now and to the Day of Eternity

"Therefore, beloved, since you look for these things, be diligent to be found by Him in peace, spotless and blameless, and regard the patience of our Lord as salvation; just as also our beloved brother Paul, according to the wisdom given him, wrote to you, as also in all his letters, speaking in them of these things, in which are some things hard to understand, which the untaught and unstable distort, as they do also the rest of the Scriptures, to their own destruction. You therefore, beloved, knowing this beforehand, be on your guard so that you are not carried away by the error of unprincipled men and fall from your own steadfastness, but grow in the grace and knowledge of our Lord and Savior Jesus Christ. To Him be the glory, both now and to the day of eternity. Amen" (2Pe. 3:14-18).

Chapter Three

IN THE BOOK OF JUDE

Through Jesus Christ Our Lord, Be Glory, Majesty, Dominion and Authority

"Now to Him who is able to keep you from stumbling, and to make you stand in the presence of His glory blameless with great joy, to the only God our Savior, through Jesus Christ our Lord, be glory, majesty, dominion and authority, before all time and now and forever. Amen" (Jude 1:24-25)

IN THE BOOK OF REVELATION

To Him Be the Glory and the Dominion Forever

"John to the seven churches that are in Asia: Grace to you and peace, from Him who is and who was and who is to come, and from the seven Spirits who are before His throne, and from Jesus Christ, the faithful witness, the firstborn of the dead, and the ruler of the kings of the earth. To Him who loves us and released us from our sins by His blood — and He has made us to be a kingdom, priests to His God and Father — to Him be the glory and the dominion forever and ever. Amen. BEHOLD, HE IS COMING WITH THE CLOUDS, and every eye will see Him, even those who pierced Him; and all the tribes of the earth will mourn over Him. So it is to be. Amen" (Rev. 1:4-7).

Chapter Three

The Living Creatures Give Glory and Honor and Thanks to Him

"After these things I looked, and behold, a door standing open in heaven, and the first voice which I had heard, like the sound of a trumpet speaking with me, said, 'Come up here, and I will show you what must take place after these things.' Immediately I was in the Spirit; and behold, a throne was standing in heaven, and One sitting on the throne. And He who was sitting was like a jasper stone and a sardius in appearance; and there was a rainbow around the throne, like an emerald in appearance. Around the throne were twenty-four thrones; and upon the thrones I saw twenty-four elders sitting, clothed in white garments, and golden crowns on their heads. Out from the throne come flashes of lightning and sounds and peals of thunder. And there were seven lamps of fire burning before the throne, which are the seven Spirits of God; and before the throne there was something like a sea of glass, like crystal; and in the center and around the throne, four living creatures full of eyes in front and behind. The first creature was like a lion, and the second creature like a calf, and the third creature had a face like that of a man, and the fourth creature was like a flying eagle. And the four living creatures, each one of them having six wings, are full of eyes around and within; and day and night they do not cease to say, 'HOLY, HOLY, HOLY is THE LORD GOD, THE ALMIGHTY, WHO WAS AND WHO IS AND WHO IS TO COME.' And when the living creatures give glory and honor and thanks to Him who sits on the throne, to Him who lives forever and ever,
10 the twenty-four elders will fall down before Him who sits on the throne, and will worship Him who lives

forever and ever, and will cast their crowns before the throne, saying, 'Worthy are You, our Lord and our God, to receive glory and honor and power; for You created all things, and because of Your will they existed, and were created'" (Rev. 4:1-11).

Worthy to Receive Power and Riches and Wisdom and Might and Honor and Glory and Blessing

"Then I looked, and I heard the voice of many angels around the throne and the living creatures and the elders; and the number of them was myriads of myriads, and thousands of thousands, saying with a loud voice, 'Worthy is the Lamb that was slain to receive power and riches and wisdom and might and honor and glory and blessing.' And every created thing which is in heaven and on the earth and under the earth and on the sea, and all things in them, I heard saying, 'To Him who sits on the throne, and to the Lamb, be blessing and honor and glory and dominion forever and ever.' And the four living creatures kept saying, 'Amen.' And the elders fell down and worshiped" (Rev. 5:11-14).

Blessing and Glory and Wisdom and Thanksgiving and Honor and Power and Might, Be to Our God

"After these things I looked, and behold, a great multitude which no one could count, from every nation and all tribes and peoples and tongues, standing before the throne and before the Lamb, clothed in white robes, and palm branches were in their hands; and they cry out with a loud voice, saying, 'Salvation to our God who sits on the throne, and to the Lamb.' And all the angels were standing around the throne and around the elders and the four living creatures; and they fell on their faces before the throne and worshiped God, saying, 'Amen, blessing and glory and wisdom and thanksgiving and honor and power and might, be to our God forever and ever. Amen''' (Rev. 7:9-12).

Gave Glory to the God of Heaven

"But after the three and a half days, the breath of life from God came into them, and they stood on their feet; and great fear fell upon those who were watching them. And they heard a loud voice from heaven saying to them, 'Come up here.' Then they went up into heaven in the cloud, and their enemies watched them. And in that hour there was a great earthquake, and a tenth of the city fell; seven thousand people were killed in the earthquake, and the rest were terrified and gave glory to the God of heaven" (Rev. 11:11-13).

He Said with a Loud Voice, Fear God, and Give Him Glory

"And I saw another angel flying in midheaven, having an eternal gospel to preach to those who live on the earth, and to every nation and tribe and tongue and people; and he said with a loud voice, 'Fear God, and give Him glory, because the hour of His judgment has come; worship Him who made the heaven and the earth and sea and springs of waters'" (Rev. 14:6-7).

Chapter Three

The Temple Was Filled with Smoke from the Glory of God and from His Power

"After these things I looked, and the temple of the tabernacle of testimony in heaven was opened, and the seven angels who had the seven plagues came out of the temple, clothed in linen, clean and bright, and girded around their chests with golden sashes. Then one of the four living creatures gave to the seven angels seven golden bowls full of the wrath of God, who lives forever and ever. And the temple was filled with smoke from the glory of God and from His power; and no one was able to enter the temple until the seven plagues of the seven angels were finished" (Rev. 15:5-8).

They Did Not Repent, so as to Give Him Glory

"The fourth angel poured out his bowl upon the sun, and it was given to it to scorch men with fire. Men were scorched with fierce heat; and they blasphemed the name of God who has the power over these plagues, and they did not repent so as to give Him glory" (Rev. 16:8-9).

Hallelujah! Salvation and Glory and Power Belong to Our God

"After these things I heard something like a loud voice of a great multitude in heaven, saying, 'Hallelujah! Salvation and glory and power belong to our God; BECAUSE HIS JUDGMENTS ARE TRUE AND RIGHTEOUS; for He has judged the great harlot who was corrupting the earth with her immorality, and HE HAS AVENGED THE BLOOD OF HIS BOND-

Chapter Three

SERVANTS ON HER.' And a second time they said, 'Hallelujah! HER SMOKE RISES UP FOREVER AND EVER.' And the twenty-four elders and the four living creatures fell down and worshiped God who sits on the throne saying, 'Amen. Hallelujah!' And a voice came from the throne, saying, 'Give praise to our God, all you His bond-servants, you who fear Him, the small and the great.' Then I heard something like the voice of a great multitude and like the sound of many waters and like the sound of mighty peals of thunder, saying, 'Hallelujah! For the Lord our God, the Almighty, reigns. Let us rejoice and be glad and give the glory to Him, for the marriage of the Lamb has come and His bride has made herself ready.' It was given to her to clothe herself in fine linen, bright and clean; for the fine linen is the righteous acts of the saints" (Rev. 19:1-8).

The Glory of God

"Then one of the seven angels who had the seven bowls full of the seven last plagues came and spoke with me, saying, 'Come here, I will show you the bride, the wife of the Lamb.' And he carried me away in the Spirit to a great and high mountain, and showed me the holy city, Jerusalem, coming down out of heaven from God, having the glory of God. Her brilliance was like a very costly stone, as a stone of crystal-clear jasper. It had a great and high wall, with twelve gates, and at the gates twelve angels; and names were written on them, which are the names of the twelve tribes of the sons of Israel. There were three gates on the east and three gates on the north and three gates on the south and three gates on the west. And the wall of the city had twelve foundation stones, and on them were the twelve names of the twelve apostles of the Lamb" (Rev. 21:9-14).

The Glory of God Has Illumined It, and Its Lamp Is the Lamb

"I saw no temple in it, for the Lord God the Almighty and the Lamb are its temple. And the city has no need of the sun or of the moon to shine on it, for the glory of God has illumined it, and its lamp is the Lamb. The nations will walk by its light, and the kings of the earth will bring their glory into it. In the daytime (for there will be no night there) its gates will never be closed; and they will bring the glory and the honor of the nations into it; and nothing unclean, and no one who practices abomination and lying, shall ever come into it, but only those whose names are written in the Lamb's book of life" (Rev. 21:22-27).

DAILY FAITH CONFESSIONS
(These are not direct quotations from the Bible but are paraphrased confessions based on scripture.)
SAY THEM OUT LOUD.

I am God's child (Jn. 1:12). I am royalty (1 Pet. 2:9). I am hidden with Christ in God (Col. 3:3). I am united with the Lord (1 Cor. 6:17). I am a friend of Christ (Jn. 15:15). I am raised up with Him, and seated with Him in heavenly places in Christ Jesus (Eph. 2:6). I was bought with a price (1 Cor. 6:19-20). I am blessed when I come in, and blessed shall I be when I go out (Deut. 28:6). I am a personal witness of Christ (Acts 1:8). I am a saint who prays in the Holy Spirit to keep myself in the love of God (Jude 1:20-21). I draw near with confidence to the throne of grace (Heb. 4:16). I have been adopted by the Father (Eph. 1:5). I am the salt and light of the earth (Mt. 5:13). I am the head and not the tail, and I am above, and not underneath. I am the lender and not the borrower (Deut. 28:13). I have authority to trample serpents and scorpions and over all the power of the enemy (Lk. 10:19). I am a member of the body of Christ (1 Cor. 12:27). God blessed me to be fruitful, and multiply, and replenish the earth, and subdue it: and have dominion (Gen. 1:28). I cannot be separated from God's love (Ro. 8:39). The good work God has begun in me will be perfected (Phil. 1:5). I can do all things through Christ who strengthens me (Phil. 4:13). No weapon that is formed against me will prosper (Is. 54:17). So then faith cometh by hearing, and hearing by the word of God (Ro. 10:17 KJV). Faith is my currency to operate in the kingdom of God (Ro. 14:23). I am God's workmanship created in Christ Jesus for good works, which God prepared beforehand (Eph. 2:10). I have been appointed to bear fruit, and that my fruit would remain (Jn. 15:16). I am being wise when I am winning souls for King Jesus (Pr. 11:30). My body is the temple of the Holy Spirit (1 Cor. 6:19). I have access to God through the Holy Spirit (Eph. 2:18). I have been justified (Ro. 5:1). Therefore there is now no condemnation for those who are in Christ Jesus (Ro. 8:1). Greater is He who is in me than he who is in the world (1 Jn. 4:4). I will do greater works than Jesus because He went to the Father (Jn. 14:12). As God was with Moses, He will be with me; God will not fail me or forsake me (Jos. 1:5). I see myself the way God see me. God sees me as a king (Gen, 17:6, Rev. 1:6) God sees me as royalty (1 Pet. 2:9). God sees me as the righteousness of God in Christ, bold as a lion (Ro. 3:22, Pr. 28:1). God sees me without spot or wrinkle because of the blood of Jesus (1 Pet. 1:19). I am having faith for big things because God owns everything and I'm His son (Ps. 24:1). No man will be able to stand before me all the days of my life (Jos. 1:5). My Father is glorified by this that I bear much fruit, and proves I'm a disciple (see Jn. 15:8). I think big and confess big things because God is big (Ps. 24:1). I will respect God for the big God that He is and my mouth will create whatever I want (Lk. 6:45). I no longer think of millions, my renewed mind thinks of billions because the wealth of the wicked is laid up for the righteous (Pr. 13:22). The sinner's job is to gather and collect for the one who is good in God's sight (Ecc. 2:26). Redemption is not complete without prosperity. Jesus hung on the cross so I can have the whole package, not just salvation (2 Cor. 8:9). I don't have to qualify, Jesus has qualified me. Jesus reversed the curse. The devil is a liar, and Jesus is the Messiah. Jesus is made unto me wisdom, righteousness, sanctification, and redemption (1 Cor. 1:30). I submit to God, I resist the devil and he flees from me (Jas. 4:7). For God has not given me the spirit of fear; but of power, and of love, and of a sound mind (2 Tim. 1:7). The Holy Spirit will teach me all things (Jn. 14:26). The Holy Spirit will guide me into all truth (Jn.16:13). The Holy Spirit abides in me, and I don't need anyone to teach me, but the anointing teaches me all things (1 Jn. 2:27). I quench fiery darts from the wicked one with the shield of faith (Eph. 6:16). I stand firm against the schemes of the devil (Eph. 6:11). I already have the victory and Satan cannot back me up. I advance and hold. Advance and hold to victory after victory (2 Cor. 2:14). I walk in love and live by faith (Gal. 5:6). I have been redeemed from the curse of the law, poverty, sickness, and spiritual death (Gal. 3:13; Deut. 28). I bear much fruit. I'm God's workmanship created beforehand for good works (Eph. 2:10). God's favor is on my life (Ps. 3:8). God blesses me and His favor surrounds me as with a shield (Ps. 5:12). The kingdom of God is within me (Lk. 17:21). I have a production plant inside of me that bears fruit to change the world (Gen. 1:28). God gives me power to get wealth to establish His covenant on earth (Deut. 8:18). I am blessed to be a blessing (Gen. 12:2). I have Satan on the run and will make a mockery of him (Jas. 4:7). No man will be able to stand before me all the days of my life (Jos. 1:5). God's angels keep me in all my ways (Ps. 91:11).

PRAYER FOR SALVATION

Say the following prayer out loud.

Heavenly Father, I am a sinner and I need a Savior. I confess Jesus Christ as the Lord of my life. I repent of all my sins. Father, I truly believe you raised Jesus from the dead. I pray this prayer in Jesus' name. Father, I am your child because Jesus is my Lord. I want to receive the fullness of the Holy Spirit. Holy Spirit come into me and fill me so I can be a mighty witness for King Jesus. I pray this prayer in Jesus' name. Amen.

PRAYER FOR BAPTISM OF THE HOLY SPIRIT

Say the following prayer out loud.

Father, I am your child because Jesus is my Lord. Jesus said, "How much more shall your heavenly Father give the Holy Spirit to those who ask Him." I ask you now in the name of Jesus to fill me with the Holy Spirit. Thank you, Father, I received the baptism of the Holy Spirit by faith. I yield my vocal organs and expect to speak in tongues as the Holy Spirit gives me utterance in Jesus name. Father, I plan to pray in the Holy Spirit building myself up on my most holy faith, and keep myself in the love of God, as mentioned in Jude 20 and 21. In Jesus name I decree it. Amen.

ABOUT THE AUTHOR

Eugene Carvalho is an administrator, Christian author of over one hundred books, and the founder of Receiving by Faith. God uses him in the offices of pastor, evangelist and prophet. He holds a bachelor's degree in biblical studies and a double minor in pastoral ministry and world missions. He also holds a master's degree in practical theology. Eugene prayed for a translator and God sent his wife Mercedes who has a six-year degree in Spanish from a university in Tampico, Mexico. They have participated in evangelism in the streets of Mexico for many years. They have also traveled to churches all over the United States and the nation of Mexico winning souls and preaching the gospel of the kingdom. Their website for their ministry is: www.receivingbyfaith.org.

BOOKS BY EUGENE IN ENGLISH

For a complete list of other books by Eugene visit receivingbyfaith.org or amazon.com.

Receiving by Faith
Faith for Every Day: 365 Daily Devotions
Faith Cometh by Hearing, and Hearing by the Word of God
Faith, Hope, and Love
Walk in Love and Live by Faith
Topical Christian Handbook and Scripture Guide
The Gospel Is the Power of God unto Salvation
Seed Time and Harvest Time
Your New Identity in Christ
The Cross and the Blood
The Holy Spirit
The Attributes of God
The Favor of God
The Glory of God
The Grace of God
The Power of God
The Promises of God
The Throne of God
The New Testament Church: A Survey from the Book of Ephesians
Vengeance and Recompense
God's Angel's
Prayer and Fasting
God's Mighty Prophets
A Survey of Jesus Through the Epistles
The Holt Spirit Will Guide You into All Truth

Old Testament Miracles
New Testament Miracles
The Fear of the Lord Is the Beginning of Knowledge; Fools Despise Wisdom and Instruction
The Psalms of David
Faith Without Works Is Dead
The Names of Jesus
Mountain Moving Confessions
In Him Was Life; and the Life Was the Light of Men
Visions and Dreams
Having Shod Your Feet with the Preparation of the Gospel of Peace
Blessed Beyond Measure
The Righteous Will Flourish like The Palm Tree
Christ Heals: What the Bible Has to Say
Jesus Is the Way, and the Truth, and the Life
My Peace I Give to You
Balancing Grace and Truth
The Old and New Testament Supernatural Acts of God Almighty
Praise and Worship Changes Everything
Understanding the Importance of Authority
If You Are Willing and Obedient
Have Faith in Jesus and the Finished Work of the Cross
Have Life More Abundantly
Pray in the Holy Spirit; Guard and Keep Yourselves in the Love of God
Sing Unto the Lord a New Song
The Power of the Tongue

The Supernatural: What the Bible Has to Say
The Truth Will Make You Free
Joy in the Holy Ghost
Praise Is Powerful: What the Bible Has to Say
Stewardship Regarding Our Finances
Love, Joy, and Peace Are Fruit of the Holy Ghost
Oh, Give Thanks to the Lord for He Is Good
The Kingdom of Heaven is at Hand
Acquiring Wisdom Is Vital
Grace and Mercy: What the Bible Has to Say
God Is Faithful: What the Bible Has to Say
God Is Love: What the Bible Has to Say
The God of Hope: What the Bible Has to Say
Pearls of Wisdom and Gems of Knowledge
Regarding Christianity
The Tongue of the Wise Uses Knowledge Aright:
But the Mouth of Fools Pours Out Foolishness
The Master's Gems
Victory is Mine, Joy is Mine, Peace Is Mine: I Told
Satan to Get Thee Behind
Striving Toward Perfection
For the Kingdom of God Is Righteousness, Peace
and Joy in the Holy Ghost
Trust and Obey: There's No Other Way
Encountering Proverbs, Ecclesiastes, and Song of
Solomon Through a Topical Survey
God's Feasts and Festivals
The Light of the Righteous Rejoices, but the Lamp
of the Wicked Goes Out
Speaking the Truth in Love
Spiritual Formation: Unleashing the Kingdom of
God within You

You Have Authority and Power: Take Back What the Devil Stole

Be Strong and Courageous

Prayer and Praise: The Big Artillery

Apostles and Prophets: The Foundation of the Church

Covenant: A Concise Survey

Sow Then Reap a Harvest

God Has Not Given Us a Spirit of Timidity, But of Power, Love, and Discipline

Blessed and Highly Favored

Grace and Peace Be Multiplied Unto You

Your Word Is a Lamp to Me Feet

John: A Key Word Study Made Simple

For Momentary, Light Affliction Is Producing For Us an Eternal Weight of Glory

Prayer Is Powerful: What the Bible Has to Say

My People Are Destroyed By Lack of Knowledge

God Deserves Pure Worship

The Mouth of the Righteous is a Fountain of Life

The Lord Requires Integrity: The Major Element of Leadership

Weeping May Last for the Night, But a Shout of Joy Comes in the Morning

A Topical Look at the Book of Deuteronomy

A Topical Look at the Book of Psalms

A Topical Look at the Book of Proverbs

A Topical Look at the Book of Isaiah

A Topical Look at the Book of John

A Topical Look at the Book of Hebrews

A Topical Look at the Book of Revelation

BOOKS BY EUGENE IN SPANISH

Las Promesas de Dios
Los Salmos de David
Lo Sobrenatural: Lo que la Bíblia Tiene que Decir
Una Mirada Topica Del Libro De Los Salmos
Dios es Amor: Lo que la Biblia Tiene que Decir
La Adquisición de la Sabiduría es Vital: Lo que la
Biblia Tiene que Decir

<u>NOTES</u>

<u>NOTES</u>

NOTES